1993

SO-BBF-339

The Utopian Moment
in Contemporary
American Poetry

The Utopian Moment
in Contemporary
American Poetry

Norman Finkelstein

Revised Edition

Lewisburg
Bucknell University Press
London and Toronto: Associated University Presses

Associated University Presses
440 Forsgate Drive
Cranbury, NJ 08512

Associated University Presses
25 Sicilian Avenue
London WC1A 2QH, England

Associated University Presses
P.O. Box 39, Clarkson Pstl. Stn.
Mississauga, Ontario,
L5J 3X9 Canada

The paper used in this publication meets the requirements
of the American National Standard for Permanence of Paper
for Printed Library Materials Z39.48-1984.

Library of Congress Cataloging-in-Publication Data

Finkelstein, Norman, 1954–
    The utopian moment in contemporary American poetry / Norman
Finkelstein. — 2nd ed.
        p.   cm.
    Includes bibliographical references and index.
    ISBN 0-8387-5247-0 (alk. paper)
    1. American poetry—20th century—History and criticism.
2. Utopias in literature.   I. Title.
PS310.U85F56   1993
811′.5409372—dc20   91-47176
                                                                  CIP

In memory
of
Harry Finkelstein
1911–1984

Do you know the mountain where, in the gloom,
The mule picks his way upon a path unknown?
In the caves the ancient dragons make their home;
And water flows over the broken stone.
Do you know the mountain? do you know it well?
It is there, O my father, that with you I would dwell.

—Goethe
(trans. Henry Weinfield)

Well, that's a proposition well composed;
the very justice of it states a demand
for some response, a further phrase, its tone
asking perhaps, or adding, or simply "yes."

It requires several voices, even assent
requires several voices, not to repeat
but to confirm if possible, to try
a variant statement in a different way, to define

in more than one direction, a moving space
constantly pushing outward, here, then there,
then there, which becomes at all because it moves,
because it holds itself to certain lines.

—William Bronk,
"Some Musicians Play
Chamber Music for Us"

The history of poetry is also a history of works which are both great and free. Whether or not it is committed in the sense required by the moment, poetry always finds its response. The mistake is to believe that the response must be immediate.

—Eugenio Montale

Contents

Preface to the Second Edition

A second edition of *The Utopian Moment in Contemporary American Poetry* affords me the opportunity to evaluate a work that is itself deeply concerned with the dynamics of literary and cultural evaluation. The fact that I have chosen not to revise, but rather to augment the first edition, should not be taken as a sign of my complete satisfaction with the book as it appeared in 1988. While I remain comfortable with the readings of individual poets and the larger claims I make for their importance, I feel the need to return to the book's title and the theoretical and historical dimensions it represents. As I state in the introduction and elaborate in chap. 1, the goal of *The Utopian Moment* is not merely to provide interpretations of a group of recent poets (some well-known, others neglected), but to place those interpretations within a coherent body of evaluative poetic criteria. These criteria are derived from certain aspects of Marxist literary criticism, and, to a lesser extent, the current debates over canon formation. In its rhetorical orientation toward the future, *The Utopian Moment* is a prospective, overreaching, even hyperbolic work. Thus it exemplifies the very principles it attempts to articulate.

If the book is to be read as an exercise in hyperbolic overreaching, then it is its utopianism that makes it so. Utopianism makes criticism extravagant, which is to say, as Harold Bloom reminds us, that the critic wanders out of bounds. Out of what bounds did I seek to wander? Two limiting orthodoxies come to mind—one Modernist, the other Postmodernist—which correspond to the two extremes in the argument over canon formation. The first of these could be called the "monumentalism" of the cultural right, a view of culture and of the canon that supports it as embodying certain timeless or universal values. Following Eliot in "Tradition and the Individual Talent," this view allows for alteration in the "existing order" but only insofar as "the main current" already flows somehow through the new work. I hope that my understanding of this relationship, which I believe to be more dialectical, allows for a clearer vision of what Ernst Bloch calls the *novum*, a quality of the new that is uncanny and anticipatory, responsive to the inchoate otherness of the future as well as the determinate past.

The second orthodoxy I sought to elude was that of leftist deconstruction, as theorized, for example, in the work of Michel Foucault. This position argues that because canons and institutions are human constructs, the values derived from them invariably are expressions of more or less coercive power. Canonic hierarchy and the power it embodies come to regarded at best as an historical expedient, at worst as an obstacle on the road to cultural liberation. Once the contingent nature of cultural and discursive authority stands revealed, any attempt to speak for the relative worth of a particular text is proof of the critic's "will to truth." Instead, the text is judged by the extent of its capitulation to the status quo, a situation in which well-intentioned criticism always appears to be "rescuing" ideologically suspect writers. Once again, I would claim that my perspective is more dialectical: beyond such endless negativity, the "bad infinity" of institutional power, the utopian moment as I envision it serves as a positive ground of values, however transitive those values might be.

Despite the fact that it seeks a middle ground in the debate over canon formation, *The Utopian Moment* is still a fiercely idealistic work. This is true not only in regard to literary theory but to recent literary history as well. Theoretically, the book posits a utopian function for criticism which operates within the ideological dimension of a literary work. In a fleeting instant of messianic stillness, the critic releases the work's cultural surplus, its anticipatory content which has come into being through the work's rigorous engagement with history. While all literary works will not yield such a surplus to the same degree (hence the evaluative power of the utopian function), I assume that all literary works are equally amenable (or resistent) to this critical treatment. But in *The Utopian Moment*, the site for this experiment is contemporary American poetry, that is, American poetry written from the fifties through the seventies, with an occasional glance backward (via the Objectivists) to the earlier Modernist period and forward to some developments of the last decade. "Moment" then refers not only to the dialectical analysis of literary texts but to a specific historical period—a period, moreover, during which American poets produce a great wealth of cultural surplus.

My task in studying these poets is to reveal this surplus and explore its utopian nature in relation to its various ideological contexts. These prevailing systems of thought and belief sometimes appear diametrically opposed to the utopian and sometimes appear as its very embodiment. No doubt it is the contradictory and heterogeneous nature of poetry in this period that makes it attractive to this sort of critical project. My work here implies that utopian thought flourishes in periods of diverse aesthetic (if not political) ideologies and cultural flux, when no unified center—whether in the form of a single movement, an individual author, or a specific locale—can be convincingly identified. But in reconsidering *The Utopian Moment* as literary history, I must also simply say, as George Oppen does in looking back on the thirties, "These were our times."

Nothing is more personal in criticism than the division of time into historical periods. By the time I graduated from college in 1975, I had begun seriously reading nearly all the poets discussed in this book. It may be true, as Bloom contends, that we are ultimately called to poetry, made into poets or readers, by a very small number of preexisting voices. These voices may be of the immediately preceding generation, but just as often they may be calling from a greater distance in time. Yet the young poet (for I was then, as now, more poet than critic) also looks around him and selects a somewhat larger number of older contemporaries for serious consideration. Many of these older figures espoused various types of oppositional poetics, derived from both Romanticism and Modernism, which, from my perspective, made them all the more attractive. And because, like so many writers of my generation, I was also embarking upon an academic career in literary studies, it was inevitable that I would seek for a more systematic understanding of those recent poets to whom I felt most drawn. Eventually, it was the Marxism of such critics as Bloch and Benjamin that provided the key to the shifting world of poetry into which I had precipitously fallen.

Today, if I also think of modern poetry through Bloom's darker wisdom, it is not because I have retreated to a merely psycho-historical position, and certainly not because Marxism has been discredited by recent world events. As a mode of historical analysis, Marxism can provide insights that are needed now more than ever as we enter a period of nearly unprecedented economic, political, and cultural fluidity. As for Bloom's psycho-historical understanding of influence, it, too, is a mode of analysis through which we may inquire into the nature of the forces that empower poets and move them to significant utterance. For criticism, the poem represents the nexus of history and personality uniquely rendered into verbal form, which appears as both complete in itself and calling for interpretive completion. No one critic can undertake the intepretation of a poem on all levels of meaning. The result, as Terry Eagleton remarks, "is more likely to lead to a nervous breakdown than a brilliant literary career." Yet when a theory such as the anxiety of influence proves to be so persuasive, we must *historicize* its rhetorical power, reading off its ideological position from its social matrix, and thereby acknowledging both its limitations and strengths. At least in this respect, literary theory must be treated in the same way in which we treat literature—not because criticism is prose poetry, as Bloom contends, but because criticism and literature are inextricably entwined in a historical narrative that all commentary furthers.

This leads me to the most recent developments in American poetry and my own work as commentator. I have always found writing about contemporary literature to be immensely exhilarating. It is an exhilaration that comes from both power and risk. To be among the first who have chosen to address a new (or seriously neglected) work of literature is to be granted a certain measure of authority that even the greatest critics of already canonized works cannot claim. On the other hand, this pleasure easily can be cancelled by the inevitable hazard of treating work which previously has gone undiscussed. Assuming that critics of contemporary literature see themselves as something more than reviewers (whose role, however honorable, is largely confined to the most immediate gestures of response), their claims for the importance of a work, however grounded in historical knowledge, always run the risk of being strongly contested and decisively overthrown in the future—or even worse, simply ignored. Here at the front, the present moment as it borders the future, there are no settled questions. We may occasionally employ the term "contemporary canon," but strictly speaking, it is a rather anxious oxymoron. If there is any consensus among the theorists of canon formation, it is that canons are the sites of a continual struggle for consensus, a struggle which is sometimes repressed and sometimes, as in the case of contemporary American poetry, quite overt.

The 1980s in American poetry saw a return to the "poetry wars" of the late fifties and sixties, with the conservative exponents of formalism and the self-conscious avant-garde of language writing both inveighing against the perceived center of slack, trivialized workshop-bred free verse which quietly dominated the seventies. The current situation has been further complicated by calls for greater literary multiculturalism, by the increasing theoretical sophistication of the poetry's largely academic readership, and the growing sense that poetry itself, at least within its traditional generic boundaries, is an outmoded discourse. The increasing fragmentation of poetic practices and of poetry's audiences would lead one to believe that even the slightest appearance of consensus has dissipated.

To a certain extent, I welcome this renewed spirit of engagement and partisanship, especially if the alternative is, as I call them in chap. 1, "narratives of diversity and accommodation." But when the poetic atmosphere heats up and critics feel called to take sides, the evaluative task gets more difficult. Because poetry wars tend to center around groups and schools rather than individual writers (the best of whom often emerge later, after the smoke has cleared), the level of critical discourse tends to be generalized and frequently reductionistic. Generalizations about a style or movement, whether put forward as manifestos written by the poets themselves or as summaries prepared by sympathetic critics, can certainly be useful both to new readers, and, later, to literary historians. It is through individual poets and their works, however, serving as the basic units of criticism, that the most successful literary and cultural assessments continue to be made—and that despite various poststructuralist claims about the death of the author. My usual method, as reflected in these pages, is to seek for those poets with determinable relationships to period styles or contemporary movements, but who at the same time succeed in distinguishing themselves through their unique deployments of language and theme.

Yet sometimes it is necessary to read more strongly against the grain. I have always felt this to be the case, for example, in my various discussions of William Bronk, including the chapter on his work in this volume. Bronk is the rare poet whose affinities to the past are extremely complex, but who has come to terms with his poetic (and philosophical) inheritance with such personal authority and rhetorical ability that he appears as a truly singular figure in his own time. Then there are the opposite situations in criticism, when the singularity of the poet must be deconstructed through the articulation of ideological connections to other poets who affect similar or sometimes apparently different stances. When individual poets are cast in such discussions, they may be seen in other constellations than those in which their fellow poets and early critics first observed them. This may help to distinguish them all the more clearly against the general literary and cultural ideologies of their time.

Readers of *The Utopian Moment* should note the additions I have made to this second version of the book. There is a new chapter on language writing ("The Utopia of Language"), which evaluates this most recent avant-garde tendency in American poetry. I have also included, as an appendix to this edition, a version of my essay on Ernst Bloch which originally appeared in *diacritics*. Bloch's view of literature is central to the poetic analyses found in this book. But his work, despite its obvious influence on as important a theorist as Fredric Jameson, has been slower to attract an American audience than that of any of his contemporaries, including Lukács, Benjamin, and Adorno. It is my hope that this situation will eventually be rectified, for Bloch's understanding of cultural processes remains as relevant today as when his work first appeared in Germany in the twenties in vastly different historical circumstances.

Acknowledgments

The first draft of this book was written with the assistance of a Faculty Development Grant from Xavier University. My thanks to the Development Committee and the university administration, and to the Reverend Robert E. Beckman, S.J., former rector of the Xavier Jesuit Community, who generously provided a quiet work place in Schott Hall, remote from busy faculty offices.

An earlier version of chapter 2 appeared in *American Poetry;* my thanks to the editor, Lee Bartlett. Likewise, the opening section of chapter 4 was published in *Sagetrieb. Sagetrieb* and the Man and Poet Series have opened their pages to me on a number of occasions: many thanks to Burton Hatlen and his colleague Carroll F. Terrell, who have been most supportive of my work.

A number of friends and colleagues read all or parts of my first draft and provided useful criticism. I am grateful to Mary DeShazer, Ernest Fontana, Henry Weinfield, and Tyrone Williams for wading through that hermetic prose. Ross Feld read the completed manuscript and provided crucial insights and support as I began my revisions. And Kathryn, my wife, listened over the course of three years to the entire book read out loud, often at the ends of long and tiring days—a true act of love.

I gratefully acknowledge the following for having given me permission to quote from published work:

Daisy Alden, for permission to quote from "The Hunter" by Frank O'Hara, which originally appeared in *Folder* 1, Tiber Press (Folder Editions), New York, 1953.

Black Sparrow Press, for permission to quote from *The Collected Books of Jack Spicer,* copyright 1975 by the Estate of Jack Spicer.

Georges Borchardt, Inc. and John Ashbery, for permission to quote from *Some Trees,* copyright 1956; *Rivers and Mountains,* copyright 1962; and *The Double Dream of Spring,* copyright 1970, by John Ashbery.

Grove Press, Inc., for permission to quote from *Meditations in an*

Emergency by Frank O'Hara, copyright 1957 by Frank O'Hara. Reprinted by permission of Grove Press. All rights reserved.

Helikon Press, 120 W. 71 Street, New York, for permission to quote from *Selected Poems & Ballads* by Helen Adam, copyright 1974 by Helen Adam.

The Jargon Society, for permission to quote from *Plum Poems* by Ross Feld, copyright 1972 by Ross Feld.

Alfred A. Knopf, Inc., for permission to quote from *The Collected Poems of Frank O'Hara*, copyright 1971 by Maureen Granville-Smith, Administratrix of the Estate of Frank O'Hara; and from *The Collected Poems of Wallace Stevens*, copyright 1957 by Wallace Stevens.

Kulchur Foundation, for permission to quote from *Turn Again to Me & Other Poems* by Helen Adam, copyright 1977 by Helen Adam.

New Directions Publishing Corporation, for permission to quote from *The Opening of the Field* by Robert Duncan, copyright 1960 by Robert Duncan; *Bending the Bow* by Robert Duncan, copyright 1968 by Robert Duncan; *Ground Work* by Robert Duncan, copyright 1984 by Robert Duncan; *The Collected Poems of George Oppen*, copyright 1965, 1967, 1968, 1972, 1974 by George Oppen; and from *Collected Poems 1909–1939* by William Carlos Williams, copyright 1938 by New Directions Publishing Corporation.

North Point Press, for permission to quote from *Life Supports*, copyright 1981 by William Bronk, published by North Point Press and reprinted by permission, all rights reserved; *Vectors and Smoothable Curves*, copyright 1983 by William Bronk; and from *Ark: The Foundations*, copyright 1980 by Ronald Johnson.

W. W. Norton & Co., for permission to quote from *The Book of the Green Man* by Ronald Johnson, copyright 1967 by Ronald Johnson; *Valley of the Many-Colored Grasses* by Ronald Johnson, copyright 1969 by Ronald Johnson; and from *All* by Louis Zukofsky, copyright 1971 by Louis Zukofsky.

The Toothpaste Press/Coffee House Press, for permission to quote from *Gone Sailing* by Helen Adam, copyright 1980 by Helen Adam.

The University of California Press, for permission to quote from *"A"* by Louis Zukofsky, copyright 1978 by Celia Zukofsky and Louis Zukofsky.

Viking Penguin Inc., for permission to quote from *Self-Portrait in a Convex Mirror* by John Ashbery, copyright 1972, 1973, 1974, 1975 by John Ashbery; *Houseboat Days* by John Ashbery, copyright 1975 by John Ashbery; *As We Know* by John Ashbery, copyright 1979 by John Ashbery; and from *A Wave* by John Ashbery, copyright 1984 by John Ashbery.

The Ecco Press for permission to quote from "The Image" and "Meditation at Lagunitas," © 1974, 1975, 1976, 1977, 1978, 1979 by Robert Hass, from *Praise* by Robert Hass.

The Utopian Moment
in Contemporary
American Poetry

Introduction: On Methodology

One of the most basic problems that criticism confronts, especially when dealing with poetry, is the unavoidably linear structure of prose discourse. Poetry, despite the fact that it is an art that occurs in time, frequently creates the impression that the totality of its utterance occurs at a single moment, all of its matter somehow experienced simultaneously. Criticism cannot hope to duplicate this effect, and thus any commentary on a poem, even of the contemporary sort that struggles for priority against the poem itself, must inevitably appear to be a hopeless (and often long-winded) act of reduction. Reduction, as Kenneth Burke informs us, can be related to the rhetorical trope of metonymy, and as Burke proceeds, "The basic 'strategy' in metonymy is this: to convey some incorporeal or intangible state in terms of the corporeal or tangible."[1] That strikes me as a fair enough description of my own basic strategy in this book, and perhaps of utopian thinking in general. If what I have to say about some specific contemporary poets, and of poetic tradition generally, appears to the reader as an illuminating metonymy for the experience of reading poetry, then I will judge my task as having been completed. After all, metonymy, as William Bronk declares in the title of his poem, is an approach to the real world.

In making this approach I have had recourse to three overlapping critical concerns: (1) explication and evaluation of some contemporary American poets and poetic "schools"; (2) exploration in the growing field of canon formation; and (3) the critique of literary ideology, both within discrete texts and throughout the social network of poetic production. Nominally then I am writing from a Marxist perspective; and indeed, I think that at the least a dialectical sensibility is required to link these three admittedly amorphous critical concerns. I say that I am writing from what is *nominally* a Marxist perspective—that is, I *name* it to be so, but I am also aware that in doing so, I leave myself open to those who say I write from what is *ostensibly* a Marxist perspective. These accusations are perhaps inevitable, perhaps even to be welcomed, given the present state of Marxist literary criticism. For my purposes, the key issue in such criticism at the moment, the issue that is implicitly and explicitly addressed throughout this book, is that of the relationship of literature to ideology. In examining this relationship, it is Ernst Bloch, of course, who most especially makes the notion of utopia his own, but utopian thinking and its relation to the ideological permeates the work of the other major figures of the Western Marxist tradition whose ideas I have used, such as Walter Benjamin, Georg Lukács, Theodor Adorno, and Herbert Marcuse. In explaining the role of utopian thought in their work, Fredric Jameson states:

> where in the older society (as in Marx's classic analysis) Utopian thought represented a diversion of revolutionary energy into idle wish-fulfillments and imaginary satisfactions, in our own time the very nature of the Utopian concept has undergone a dialectical reversal. Now it is practical thinking which everywhere represents a capitulation to the system itself, and stands as a testimony to the power of the system to transform even its adversaries into its own mirror image. The Utopian idea, on the contrary, keeps alive the possibility of a world qualitatively distinct from this one and takes the form of a stubborn negation of all that is.[2]

Terry Eagleton has recently called this concept and the critical strategies that emerge from it into question. Considering the lack of a radical working class tradition in the United States, in comparison to the situation in England, Eagleton observes that

> The unusual popularity of the various Hegelian inflections of Marxism in the USA is surely to be seen, not only as a particularly appropriate "answer" to a thoroughly commodified society, but as part of the problem—the reflex of a condition in which the commodity bulks so large that it threatens to obfuscate, not only bourgeois social relations, but a specifically political and institutional understanding in areas of the Left.[3]

But if Lukács, Adorno, Marcuse, and others have themselves suffered commodification at the hands of the institutionalized Left (*is* there such a thing?), this in itself cannot preclude the continued attempt to appropriate their ideas for the contemporary demands of literary criticism—as Eagleton himself has demonstrated in his fine book on Walter Benjamin.

But it is in an earlier work of Eagleton, *Criticism and Ideology*, that we find one of the few thoroughgoing attempts to offer a cohesive theory of Marxist literary criticism. It is by no means my intention to offer a complete critique of that work, but rather point out those concepts developed therein which have most affected my own work in poetic analysis and canon formation. A number of these concepts, at least in broad outline, seem crucial to any serious examination of literature and ideology: for example, the structuration of a uniquely aesthetic ideology that is related both to the general ideology of a given society and a specifically literary mode of production. Yet if we consider that ideology, in Marx's original sense of the term, is synonymous with "false consciousness"; and Eagleton's contention that, despite the deformative effect of literary texts upon ideological structures, *literature is primarily constituted by ideology,* we encounter one of the few troubling flaws in his work. A careful reading of *The German Ideology* will reveal that at no point do Marx and Engels apply their definition of the ideological to the aesthetic sphere, though they take great pains to include political, legal, philosophical and religious systems in the working-through of that definition.[4] Nearly all of Marx's actual references to art and ideology are fragmentary and ambiguous, and have been examined by Cliff Slaughter in his attempt to refute "those interpreters of Marx who explicitly view literature as ideology (or as a production which works on and enables us to see ideology)."[5] Slaughter concludes:

> This is the sense in which art constitutes a reality which is not mere ideology. To be realistic, art and literature do not merely describe the immediate data of experience, and certainly not only the ideological categories with which they are comprehended. What is essential is that the meaning of the human struggle to transcend this experience and this ideology is wrested *from* the forms of appearance, *from* ideology, and presented to men and women in such a way that they prepare, in whatever way their lives demand and make possible, to survive and overcome them.[6]

The struggle that Slaughter describes could certainly be related to the "spirit of Utopia" that Bloch has observed not only in "idealist" works of art, but in the materialistic theories of Marx himself. And yet the utopian or "messianic" interpretations of Marxism by Bloch, Benjamin and Marcuse continue to be regarded with suspicion by those modern critics who seek to rid literary theory of any last vestiges of its metaphysical bias. One can only reply that if Marx, in his critique of religion, sought to "pluck the living flower," modern criticism would uproot the entire bed, without distinguishing the blossoms from the weeds.

Given these considerations, readers should be alert to the nuances in my use of the term "ideology," especially when it appears in analyses of recent poetry. When I consider the range of styles and voices of today's "poetry scene," I am quickly convinced of the accuracy of Eagleton's category of "aesthetic ideology." Indeed, does Postmodernism itself fall into such a category? Gerald Graff seems to think so, and there is no more chastening experience for the devotee of contemporary culture than even a quick glimpse at the "rhetorical scoreboard" of aesthetic values that he offers in *Literature Against Itself.*[7] Graff's analysis of the guilt by association practiced by Postmodern writers and critics is undeniably accurate, if not as extensive as he claims; but this certainly does not *negate* the value of indeterminacy, immediacy, process, etc., as historically appropriate strategies when specifically applied in an act of artistic realization. What Graff suggests, or at least implies, is that the *reification* of those values into an ideology—a false, limited, preconceived view of changing material circumstances—is detrimental to the continued tradition of art as an expression of human knowledge. What makes the current situation all the more ironic is the reification of a set of values originally conceived to free the writer from the artificial, superannuated constraints of aesthetic dogma—specifically, those that go under the general rubric of the New Criticism. The sort of formalism in both poetry and criticism supported by the New Critical pantheon has long given way to an updated version of the Battle of the Books, some aspects of which I have examined in chapter 1. In the midst of such rapid changes, any Marxist engaged in evaluative procedures obviously must recall the fate of Georg Lukács during the Stalinist period, before his opponents remind him of the same. On the other hand, I wholly endorse Graff (who has made good use of Lukács) when, in defending his book, he declares:

> Licenses to practice epistemological revolution are now as available as handguns, of course, and any textual leftist can set himself up in the business by claiming his peculiar form of linguistic sport threatens the ruling class.[8]

But the attitude expressed in such a statement is actually to be found much less in this book than the far more generous spirit of restorative hermeneutics with which Ernst Bloch may be most closely identified.[9] The analyses of individual poets that make up the bulk of this volume should be regarded in just this spirit, keeping in mind, of course, that a deliberate but hardly programmatic attempt at canon formation is simultaneously under way. Arguably, there is not a single poet discussed here whose canonical status is not in some way problematic. Some have attracted a good deal of critical attention; others have received virtually none at all. I have discussed or at least alluded to the reasons for this situation in each chapter, but I have also attempted to quote amply yet judiciously, so that readers, if they are not familiar with a particular poet, will be able to follow the movement of my argument as well as draw some of their own conclusions. Walter Benjamin once dreamed of "writing" a book made up entirely of quotations, and while I appreciate the utopian ideal encoded in that dream, I still acknowledge the prohibitive habits of critical discourse which encircle, if not violate, the chosen quotes. This is another basic problem of criticism, so let us say only that this book, by weaving those poems into its argumentative fabric, "is shot through with chips of Messianic time."[10]

At the Front: Evaluating Contemporary Poetry

Also the Golden Age was a dark time
if there was one. I think it is now and was not
ever. It is dark now as it always was.

—William Bronk

The men in the kitchens
Their women in the foundries
The children in the wars
The old men at the boundaries.

—Louis Zukofsky

The myth of the Golden Age is as seductive to literary critics as it is to any other group of historically oriented intellectuals. It is fitting then that a poem, which is ordinarily considered the object of critical inquiry, should be used occasionally as the vehicle for self-criticism. This is especially true for a critic who addresses himself to contemporary poetry, for in constructing a narrative based on recent texts, I am frequently tempted to declare, in a tone invariably laden with authority, that in such a poet, such a school, such a period, some modern equivalent of the Golden Age is to be found. In fact, there will be moments in this book when I will indeed make such claims: but rather than appear to be yielding to temptation, I can only hope that my application of that quality of thought and feeling which has been called utopian will be convincing, given the gradual development of my concomitant theoretical model. But in quoting the opening lines of William Bronk's "About Dynamism, Desire and Various Fictions," I refer at present to a somewhat different, more conventionally temporal notion of the Golden Age: I mean the privileged moments in literary history when it appears that various social conditions are so arranged as to produce a truly exemplary body of works. To argue for the converse, of course, is an equally strong temptation: that was the worst of times, a genuine Dark Age, and it has now become apparent how such powers as were conspired to create such dismaying circumstances. Bronk's poem relieves us of that critical burden (though as we shall see, it imposes others), in that we become conscious of our historical prejudices, and thus of the relative limits of our narrative abilities. Bronk, more extreme than any critic can afford to be, dismisses all forms of historical narrative, embracing a radically ahistorical position in which all ages are equally dark—or golden. "The beautiful is that, nothing more," the poet goes on to say, at times even resting content in such knowledge. The critic, restless by virtue of his need to define, instead continually seeks to make historical evaluations, despite the vexing questions such attempts always raise.

The extraordinary diversity that characterizes American poetry since World War II, and the speed with which such diversity has come to be, has been noted and studied for some time now, and has been related, logically enough, to the same qualities we find in American culture at large. Critics have, for the most part, avoided claims for a Golden Age or a Dark Age, arguing instead, especially in recent studies, for a middle level of poetic achievement. The most comprehensive of these studies, James Breslin's *From Modern to Contemporary*, presents the history of postwar American poetry as an alternation between exhaustion and revitalization, conflict and compromise. By the end of this judicious and informed narrative, we are offered this encapsulated scenario:

> If American poetry in the middle fifties resembled a peaceful public park on a pleasant summer Sunday afternoon, and if by the early sixties it had been transformed into a war zone, the air heavy with manifestos, then by the early 1980s the atmosphere has lightened and the scene more resembles a small affluent town in Northern California.[1]

And Breslin concludes that "without a strong central authority, the current period possesses a kind of heterogeneous unity whose diversity supports vitality."[2] Robert Von Hallberg would probably agree. The concluding chapter of his ambitious *American Poetry and Culture 1945–1980* is called "Suburbs," and like the residents of Breslin's Northern California town, the writers with whom Von Hallberg is concerned end up offering, after a generation of conflict and doubt, a poetry "of accommodation rather than opposition."[3] Then there is Charles Altieri, who, having already considered the more extreme poetry of the sixties in his *Enlarging the Temple*, says of poetry in the seventies that "most poets are not as concerned with a series of interrelated explorations of abstract ideas as they are with bringing single poems to complex rhetorical resolutions."[4] After describing a number of the paradigms for recent composition, Altieri, like a number of his fellows, puts forward John Ashbery as the "major poet of our minor age."[5]

There are notable exceptions, however, to this scrupulous care on the part of most critics to avoid large claims of any sort for recent poetry. One turns with both trepidation and excitement to Charles Newman's *The Post-Modern Aura,* a book primarily devoted to fiction and theory, but containing one small, withering chapter on poetry. For Newman, the narrative of opposition and accommodation traced by Breslin or Von Hallberg is almost beside the point: when the critical terms necessary for a coherent historical analysis have become inflated beyond use or recognition, genuine cultural conflict collapses due to the "intrinsic devaluation of all received ideas."[6] Any opposition to prevailing cultural norms—a prerequisite for the historical narrative of recent poetry— must actually be seen as "rooted in a critique of culture so fully assimilated that it can no longer claim any adversary moral or political authority."[7] No wonder then that when Newman considers poetry, he sees "an aspect of literature commissioned expressly for the margin," "content to settle for idle conversation."[8] Against all prevailing descriptive models, Newman concludes that

> Post-Modern poetry is neither concrete nor mystical, but has become the least allusive and most predictable form of contemporary literature; a true shorthand based not upon compression but the contemporary preference for abbreviation—a scenario for untransmitted feelings, exemplifying above all a time which exceeds the artist's understanding.[9]

This is a return to the myth of the Dark Age with a vengeance. But what makes Newman's indictment so appealing (aside from his unfailing wit) is that, through his mordant articulation of the current situation, we can see evidence of this same failing in contemporary poetry in the observations of those critics who for the most part provide a positive assessment of recent work. In other words, Newman's thoroughgoing critique helps us recognize the only partly hidden anxieties of other critics in regard to their chosen subject. For example, after considering the work of a group of poets who write within the bounds of the "scenic style," Altieri states that

> the dominant impression is of a sense of person constructed around self-confident self-pity and yet still confined to polishing the small change. These poets are fairly young, but at about their age Eliot had produced *The Waste Land;* Stevens, *Harmonium;* and Pound, *A Draft of Thirty Cantos.*[10]

And in a similar analysis, Alan Williamson takes us "to the nadir of the contemporary poetry of the self, in a poetry that finds the personal self sterile, perhaps not even there, yet can posit no escape from it either by plunging into a fertile collective unconscious or by taking an interest in the outside world."[11] Even Von Hallberg, whose central thesis is that American poetry has successfully spoken from the sense of a cultural center, asserts that "empires are not made or broken by poems, but through poetry they are remembered and even justified. During the decade after the war, and since, there has been a demand in America for cultural coherence that helps ratify imperium."[12] This observation seems to me so calculatedly ambivalent as to make one see the critic as a minor courtier remarking unconfidently about the Emperor's new clothes.

It is one of the major premises of this book that poets who make peace with their age are bound to impose ultimately disabling ideological limitations upon their enterprises. The same may be said for critics who, despite whatever sophisticated methodologies they may employ, produce narratives of diversity and accommodation. I would sooner address Newman's furious vision of an utterly marginal poetry than any of a number of analyses of middle registers, narcissistic selves, and imperial apologists. It is because of just such a response as mine, of course, that critics of contemporary poetry have recognized that any discussion of the current situation must lead through an understanding of canon formation to the invention (or rediscovery) of a ground of values that allow for clearly articulated judgments. This, however, does not mean a return to the ideological "poetry wars" of the sixties, that by now have been thoroughly documented. As Newman persuasively argues, "an inflationary culture, because its overlapping realities are not only pro- liferating but cancelling each other out, tends to polarize theories as it recirculates them."[13] Nevertheless, I cannot see how we can avoid the principles of *real* conflict and change (pace Bronk), which for my pur- poses can be equated with what Fredric Jameson calls "the Dialectic of Utopia and Ideology." Against the easygoing relativism and quiescence of the current situation, I call to mind Zukofsky's brief lyric, the second epigraph of this chapter, which seems to speak now of both political and literary conflict: poets and critics seem both children in the wars and old men at the boundaries: the wars of ideology and canon, the boundaries of the present moment.

Such boundaries call to mind Ernst Bloch's conception of "the front," "the farthest section of time, where we find ourselves living and ac- tive."[14] At the front we bring to bear all our powers and project our- selves forward into the anticipated future. At the same time however, we are at our weakest at the front; our means of judging what is coming into being is always inadequate. As Bloch says, "The unique point of con- vergence of past, present and future cultures is a human content that is nowhere as yet adequately manifest, but can certainly be appropriately anticipated."[15] Although we cannot make exact canonical judgments, we must still attempt to make decisions that in retrospect may be deemed "appropriately anticipated." One means of doing that is through Bloch's concept of a cultural surplus,

> something that moves above and beyond the ideology of a particular age. Only this "plus" persists through the ages, once the social basis and ideology of an epoch have decayed; and remains as the substrate that will bear fruit and be a heritage for other times. This substrate is essentially utopian, and the only notion that accords with it is the utopian-concrete concept.[16]

The obvious risk in adopting this strategy lies in the subjectivity of the utopian concept, which is rarely as concrete as Bloch wishes. Jameson, extrapolating from Bloch's idea, takes us a step further by calling for a Marxist hermeneutic that "negatively" demystifies the ideological content of cultural objects and "positively" exposes their "simultaneously Utopian power as the symbolic affirmation of a specific historical and class form of collective unity."[17] This notion provides us with the beginning of a critical methodology, but still remains vague—for how do we know that a particular ideological expression is actually to be seen as an affirmation, and therefore as utopian? How are we to interpret, say, Ronald Johnson's neo-Romanticism in *The Book of the Green Man*, a poem that appears to be premised upon a nostalgic desire for an outmoded discourse? What of the austerity of William Bronk's poetry, replete with philosophical contradictions? How do both compare to John Ashbery's "magma of interiors," in which multiple discourses are deliberately appropriated to achieve an endless, leveled surface of language? Are we to sift through such different bodies of work, claiming one feature as mere ideology, another as utopian affirmation?

My answer is a qualified yes. Just as Walter Benjamin instructed his historical materialist to brush history against the grain, to blast a specific era out of the homogeneous course of history, to recuperate a version of the past which is shot through with chips of Messianic time, so too the critic of contemporary literature must seek utopian insights. For today as many images of the present flit by as of the past, at a speed that even Benjamin himself could not have imagined. Some of these images—that is, texts—may disappear into the margins. Others may be canonized, but through processes that are highly suspect. In either event we will be aided in our task when we remember that, as Terry Eagleton says,

> the "truth" of the text is not an essence but a practice—the practice of its relation to ideology, and in terms of that to history. On the basis of this practice, the text constitutes itself as a structure: it destructures ideology in order to reconstitute it on its own relatively autonomous

terms, in order to process and recast it in aesthetic production, at the same time it is itself destructured to variable degrees by the effect of ideology upon it.[18]

I envision the task of the critic in dealing with contemporary poetry, then, as decidedly dialectical: his analysis must allow for the simultaneous preservation, negation, and elevation (*aufhebung*) of specific moments within the text as responsive to historical knowledge. Arguably, this is what texts themselves do to the matter of which they are constituted; and as Eagleton indicates, the critic must enter into the practice of the text, reading off its relations to ideology and noting the formal and thematic means by which it establishes its autonomous identity. In much of what follows, it is the poem's autonomy that comes to be associated with the utopian propensity, for as we have seen Jameson observe, the utopian idea "keeps alive the possibility of a world qualitatively distinct from this one and takes the form of a stubborn negation of all that is." If such a description seems outlandish in the face of what is commonly understood about the Objectivists or the poets of the New York School, I must, at this point, beg the reader's forbearance. As Frank and Fritzie Manuel say at the beginning of their great historical study, *Utopian Thought in the Western World:*

> The bypassing of a rigid definition may distress some philosophical intelligences who demand that at the opening of an inquiry its terms be spelled out in contractual language; but as the whole of this work is intended to endow the idea of utopia with historical meaning, those looking for a dictionary label or a pat phrase had better try elsewhere. Utopia acquires plural meanings in the course of our study, in which we presuppose the existence of a utopian propensity in man as William James in his famous lectures assumed a "religious propensity" while pointedly refusing to define religion. . . . The utopian propensity is no more equally distributed among men in all times and places than the religious propensity, though it is doubtful whether anyone is totally devoid of it. There may even be a utopian vocation.[19]

It remains to be seen how these concepts may interact with the analyses of contemporary poetry and of canon formation that provided our point of departure. As I have implied, these areas of study are linked: to evaluate contemporary poetry, even to review a single volume in isolation, is to participate (however unconsciously) in the ongoing process of canon formation, which is to articulate a particular literary ideology. Most scholars who have addressed one or another of these subjects argue that "canon is not a literary category but a category of power." Thus there are "texts that are forceful in a given situation and those which are not."[20] Focusing specifically on contemporary poetry, Altieri observes that "a mode becomes dominant when the ethos it idealizes develops institutional power—both as a model for the ways in which agents represent themselves and, more important, as the basic example of what matters in reading and in attributing significance to what one reads."[21] If this is the case, then the establishment of a canon, or rather, any claim to canonic status, is an attempt to set boundaries within which readers, critics, editors, and others conduct normative literary transactions— consuming new books, following certain journals, analyzing the works of given authors, making publishing decisions, awarding prizes, and the like. On one level, canons create the illusion of the status quo, which is to say that canon formation is part of the larger ideological apparatus of a given society: that part of the apparatus that functions with specific regard to the intellectual elite. As Von Hallberg asserts:

> The most ambitious literary critics, who know they can help mold ideology, set themselves the task of constructing a canon. . . . Critics who build canons deliberately fight not for a list of poets only, but for a proper audience whose taste is formed correctly rather than eclectically. For Wordsworth, literary taste was not easily separable from "our moral feelings." Canonists worry about what will enable a community of readers to distinguish first-rate from second-rate thought and expression. A national canon stands as proof that such distinctions can be made so as to command assent; that the nation asks from its writers support for its policies, at the very least its educational policies; that one national objective is to preserve, by education, a hold on the past and a claim on the future.[22]

Such analyses of canon formation remain problematic insofar as they are primarily descriptive; they imply a critique of an ideological apparatus, but do not necessarily call for its dismantling. On the other hand, whether it is even possible "to disrupt the canonical economy as such, the dynamics of cultural authority,"[23] is very much an open question, given the way in which alternative positions tend to become reified and even assimilated under our present socio-economic conditions. There is no mistaking the urgency of these issues, however. Eagleton is particularly strong on this point:

> But it is not only a question of the ideological use of a particular literary work; it is, more fundamentally, a question of the ideological significance of the cultural and academic institutionalisation of literature as such. What is finally at stake is not literary texts but Literature—the ideological significance of the process whereby certain historical texts are severed from their social formations, defined as "literary," bound and ranked together to constitute a series of "literary traditions" and interrogated to yield a set of ideologically presupposed responses.[24]

If such is the case, then the critic must stand simultaneously within and without the structure of the canonical economy. A negative critique of canon formation must always be prepared to speak against the tendency to install reified cultural monuments, especially if "canon formation has a particular function in an empire."[25] A positive evaluation of given texts must inevitably take place within the canonical economy, though it is to be hoped that the self-consciousness granted to us by the recent study of canon will make us examine our own value systems with the utmost care.

Thus it should be clear that when I offer the utopian propensity as a positive value, a quality which enables me to argue for the worth of a particular poet and even elevate him or her to canonic status, I do so with an understanding that a thorough "working through" of the text is always necessary, so that we may enter finally into the historical dimension, that place where one may witness the text's dialogue with the literary and social history from which it springs. In the case of American poetry, this is a dialogue conducted in recent years in a bewildering diversity of voices and terms. In art the utopian category has never been exclusively political or even social in its direct expression; personal, inward and existential texts maintain the power of the possible as much as works more obviously grounded in immediate social circumstances. But for Bloch and similar thinkers, the utopian propensity is always a matter of tendency, of orientation and direction. This is why Bloch uses the metaphor of a horizon in discussing the future, and Benjamin the metaphor of a gate. Cognition gives way to anticipation here, and the analytic mode of discourse abruptly becomes rhapsodic. Literary criticism cannot be conducted through intuition, of course; but it is equally misguided to allow prevailing literary standards alone to determine questions of worth. Arguably, a poem that achieves genuine historical moment will have fully subsumed those antecedents and/or contemporaries of greatest relevance to it. This is why Eagleton argues for an understanding of the text as a practice, although it presents itself at first and makes its strongest emotional claims as a free or autonomous entity, qualitatively different—new. And as Hans Robert Jauss observes,

> The new is thus not only an *aesthetic* category. . . . The new also becomes a *historical* category when the diachronic analysis of literature is pushed further to ask which historical moments are really the ones that first make new that which is new in a literary phenomenon; to what degree this new element is already perceptible in the historical instant of its emergence; which distance, path or detour of understanding were required for its realization in content, and whether the moment of its full actualization was so influential that it could alter the perspective on the old, and thereby the canonization of the literary past.[26]

In considering contemporary poetry, critics must always take into account Jauss's "distance, path or detour of understanding," for such routes usually lead to the margins rather than any supposed center. Critics must often lead the work back along these paths to "the moment of full actualization." Furthermore, because they are conscious of the new as a historically determined category rather than a seemingly arbitrary appearance, they will be more receptive to those crucial works "that at the moment of their appearance are not yet directed at any specific audience, but that break through the familiar horizon of literary expectation so completely that an audience can only gradually develop for them."[27] Nor is it only recent theorists who have had such insights. Yeats, writing of Blake after a century of relative neglect, declares that "there have been men who loved the future like a mistress, and the future mixed her breath into their breath and shook her hair about them, and hid them from the understanding of their times."[28]

This then is a model of canon formation that certainly involves notions of power and ideology, but in such a way as to subvert as much as reinforce received images of canonic authority. The idea of a literary canon is neither preserved nor cancelled; rather, the dialectical play of freedom and authority, as it is encoded in the text, and then in a sequence of texts (a tradition) is understood as a legible presence. What *is* cancelled is the notion of canon as *immergleich:* Benjamin's vision of history as "ever-the-same," homogeneous, empty and complicit in the maintenance of the status quo. The utopian propensity as a measure of value, the positive ground demanded of literary criticism by the study of canon formation, provides a response to the serious challenge presented by writers such as Newman, who see poetry today as little more than a self-indulgent and trivializing expression of individual paralysis. Those poets in whom the utopian consciousness is most active are by no means victimized by an inability to understand their time: the various "practices" of which their poetry consists place them both in and beyond their time, which partly accounts for the frequent lack of serious critical attention that has been paid them. Furthermore, despite their literary affiliations or convenient placement in one or another school of poetry, these figures are almost invariably resistant to analysis in terms of a period style—as many recent critics have conducted upon many recent poets, more or less consciously demonstrating the ways they merely meet rather than work upon prevailing audience expectations. Their language submerged in the discourse of the moment, their emotional capacities deformed by a set of stock responses to experience, these are the poets who produce, in Jauss's term, "culinary" works of art. Instead, the compelling otherness I seek in contemporary poetry, if it is to be perceived within the canonical economy, must be addressed not in terms of pluralism or even of relativistic "counter-history," but as a ghostly afterlife of language, a resonance that comparatively few poets of any age are able to incorporate into their utterance. As Jack Spicer instructs us, however obscurely:

> Hold to the future. With firm hands.
> The future of each afterlife, of each ghost,
> of each word that is about to be mentioned.[29]

The irony here is that one cannot grasp the future firmly; as Bloch says, it is a perpetual "not yet." The historical relevance of the autonomous text is never immanent; it is always delayed, projected forward to a horizon which we are always just approaching. Poetry of this sort (and Spicer's work is a perfect example) is a "prefiguring," and there is often a price to pay when poetry attains to such conditions. As Theodor Adorno reminds us,

> the greatest fetish of cultural criticism is the notion of culture as such. For no authentic work of art and no true philosophy, according to their very meaning, has ever exhausted itself in itself alone, in its being-in-itself. They have always stood in relation to the actual life-process of society from which they have distinguished themselves. Their very rejection of the guilt of a life which blindly and callously reproduces itself, their insistence on independence and autonomy, on separation from the prevailing realm of purposes, implies, at least as an unconscious element, the promise of a condition in which freedom were realized. This remains an equivocal promise of culture as long as its existence depends on a bewitched reality and, ultimately, on control over the work of others.[30]

Adorno approaches the heart of the problem for any critic of contemporary poetry who is conscious of matters of ideology and canon in his evaluative procedures. Because cultural production takes place under the veil of ideology ("a bewitched reality"), in a society which depends on exploitation for its material existence ("control over the work of others"), then cultural products, including new poetry, will offer only "an equivocal promise." The autonomy of the poem, or of the critical methodology applied to it, may well signify "the promise of a condition in which freedom were realized." But the price of such freedom is exceedingly high, and the rejection of guilt that Adorno describes is never fully achieved. The alienation of the artist and intellectual has long since become both a commodity and a source of false pride, but for all that it remains a decisive force in evaluating new art.[31] When does the apparent autonomy of a poetic stance signify a utopian space that has opened in the midst of our present claustrophobic world—the world that George

Oppen, for example, scrutinizes in *Of Being Numerous?* When, on the other hand, is autonomy merely an alienated gesture, and the parading of alienation itself a capitulation rather than an implied critique? One wonders how many poets today could honestly say along with William Bronk, as he does in "The Abnegation,"

> . . . that my want's agony declare
> that such as we want has nothing to say to the world;
> if the world wants, it nothing wants for us.[32]

Major poets have always taken such risks as Bronk or Oppen do; and it seems that since the onset of those conditions that led to Romanticism, if not before, the risk most often taken has been that of lofty separation and radical interiority.[33] More recently, an equally radical alternative has arisen: the plunge of poetry into the immediacies of time and space that we associate variously with Pound, Williams and their followers.[34] Indeed, it can be argued that the fragmentation that marks contemporary American poetry results from the movement between these interiorizing and exteriorizing discourses; this tension has led in turn, perhaps inevitably, to the postwar schisms that scholars have by now so carefully described. This movement between interiority and exteriority has strongly affected my own sense of poetic value, and has contributed to my choice of the poets discussed in the following chapters. Thus I begin by considering the Objectivists, for whom the immediate experience of the exterior world is both a thematic ideal and a technical challenge. Next I consider the poetry of Ashbery and O'Hara, in which lingering traces of a crucial interiorizing mode—the Romantic sublime—is played off against a dominant language of surfaces. Romantic interiority also plays an important role in my longest chapter, on various figures associated with the San Francisco Renaissance, where this mode often appears in strange syntheses with Modernist strategies. Finally, I offer a reading of William Bronk, the one contemporary poet most directly concerned with the notion of historicity, a concern which leads him beyond interior and exterior modes to a more direct, though insistently contradictory argument with utopian desire itself. Each of my analyses is meant to be read as a "working through" of the poetry, in which the practice of the text in relation to literary ideologies and prevailing modes of discourse is gradually revealed; and likewise its unique adumbration of the utopian propensity, the means by which the poem, to use George Oppen's phrase, maintains its access to "the metaphysical sense / Of the future."

I end this chapter with another quote from *Of Being Numerous.* "It is difficult now to speak of poetry—" warns Oppen, typically understating his case—

about those who have recognized the range of choice or those who have lived within the life they were born to—. It is not precisely a question of profundity but a different order of experience. One would have to tell what happens in a life, what choices present themselves, what the world is for us, what happens in time, what thought is in the course of a life and therefore what art is, and the isolation of the actual.[35]

The dialectical rhythms of thought that may be detected in the work of a poet like Oppen, a poet whose personal and literary biography is central to the history of poetry in our time, can often provide us with a means of assessing our current poetic circumstances. Poets are those "who have recognized the range of choice," not "those who have lived within the life they were born to"; and critics, in speaking of poetry, must tell "what choices present themselves." Throughout Oppen's exemplary work, "what happens in a life" always must be associated with "what the world is for us, what happens in time." Only in this way can we hope to perceive—and perhaps even reach—"a different order of experience."

What Was Objectivism?

No symbolism can be permitted to obscure the real purpose, to lift the world of the senses to the level of the imagination and so give it new currency.[1]

—William Carlos Williams,
"Against the Weather"

Determining the exact historical content of a given aesthetic ideology is a difficult and often bitter task. For artists' rationalizations of their work are more often sets of strategies than bodies of preconceived beliefs. When these strategies are successful, we tend to forget about them—and why not? We are in the presence of the Beautiful, which, as Keats says, "obliterates all considerations." But because this privileged moment never comes to us alone, but rather, with all its historical baggage dragged behind it, we inevitably question its luminous presence. And thus we are led to discover how that luminous presence, the aura of the work, appears in a dialectical relationship with the historical conditions that produced it.

For Walter Benjamin, the work's aura is always a matter of ritualized distance. In modern times, we self-consciously perceive the aura (which is to say, it becomes a critical category) because of its decay, which is a result of the loss of distance between us and the object. In the same way the distance between the viewer and the painting is lessened by the mechanical reproduction of photography and the special interpretative relationship between listener and storyteller is violated by the increased reliance on the information industry and its prompt verifiability of "the news." Baudelaire is the representative modern poet because he recognizes that the figure of the poet no longer commands a ritual distance from his audience; his halo is lost, and his poetry acknowledges that loss and the concomitant difficulty a modern reader will have with traditional lyricism. In all these cases it is the masses with their desire "to bring things 'closer' spatially and humanly" that are implicated in the decay of the aura; artistic production is no longer based on ritual, but on politics.[2] These ideas are crucial to an understanding of Objectivism.

In the previous chapter I tried to establish that one means of evaluating contemporary poetry—that is, of making canonical judgements—depends on gauging the extent and quality of the poem's engagement with those historical forces that allow for its production. Such an act of measurement appears relatively feasible, from our present perspective, when we consider major texts of the Romantic and Modernist periods. *The Prelude, Prometheus Unbound, In Memoriam;* or *The Wasteland, The Cantos,* even *Notes Toward a Supreme Fiction:* these poems, as challenging as they are, are open to an analysis that takes into account their aesthetic ideologies and allows for their auras to be successfully recuperated in the light of their historical preconditions. What do we do, however, with a poetry that, in a gesture at least as radical as Baudelaire's, seems deliberately to renounce its claim to an aura, or radically transforms the premises upon which such a claim has been traditionally built? Objectivist poetry is such a body of work, in that the privileged moment seems to be derived not from a ritual or interior impulse but an exterior object or event that carries aesthetic worth prior to the poet's work of creation, or indeed, of perception itself. The poem, as an act of attention, focuses the consciousness, making it more receptive to external, objective phenomena within a momentary span of time. It is the poet's task, as Williams says in *Spring and All* (1923),

> to perfect the ability to record at the moment when the consciousness is enlarged by the sympathies and the unity of understanding which the imagination gives, to practice skill in recording the force moving, then to know it, in the largeness of its proportions.[3]

In the theoretical statements of Williams and his followers, the revolutionary principles of Pound's Imagist Manifesto (direct treatment of the "thing," strict linguistic economy, rhythm as a musical phrase) are stripped of their aestheticized trappings and set into motion. Williams's attack on "the beautiful illusion" in *Spring and All* marks a definite break with what Hugh Kenner calls, in contrasting Williams and Wallace Stevens, "the elevated verse of the Noble Rider."[4] But to break with such verse, which signifies a break with the Romantic notion of the sublime as well, means, at first glance, a deliberate renunciation of historical matter within the poem. The Objectivists' desire to return to the immediate and the particular seems to shut out an engagement with history as the motive force of the poem. Confined to a narrow, even impoverished set of concerns ("'out of poverty / to begin // again'" Oppen will later sing), the Objectivists willfully deny the plenitude of Romantic interiority, a mode of discourse which permitted the poets a means of gathering history into the symbolic contours of their verse; thus sustaining their auratic power. Pound, and to some extent Yeats, as direct heirs to this mode, take history itself as their subject; the voices of *The Cantos,* or on a different scale, "Easter 1916" and "The Second Coming" seem to have merged so thoroughly with historical matter that a version of History (engineered through ideology, of course) appears to be speaking itself. But the Objectivists choose instead to be men in the world:

> I cannot even now
> Altogether disengage myself
> From those men
>
> With whom I stood in emplacements, in mess tents,
> In hospitals and sheds and hid in the gullies
> Of blasted roads in a ruined country[5]

Here we confront the central tension of Objectivism: in a world in which immediate particulars have come to bear the sign of history as never before, in an America in which capitalism has left no sphere of human activity free of its homogenizing ideologies of imperialism and consumerism, Objectivism, as the term has come to be used, must ultimately be considered nothing more than a pleasant critical myth. The various statements of the Objectivists, and certainly their poetries, attest to this fact. Indeed, even the struggle for objectivity, as may be witnessed in the work of such poets as Williams, Zukofsky and Oppen, indicates the palpable presence of a self-conscious subject actively seeking entrance into a realm "of mere being"—a realm that ceases to exist, if it ever did, when it becomes the focal point of poetic desire. Zukofsky's "totality of perfect rest," Williams's "no ideas but in things," Oppen's "test of truth" are all utopian tropes for a poetry capable of reconciling the immediate particulars of the world as given with "the will to change" or historical process, which, as Charles Olson rightly declares, is at the heart of any creative endeavor. The reconciliation of these opposing tendencies becomes the preeminent task of American poetry as it enters its most recent stage of development.

There are numerous moments in the works of the Objectivists when the world appears perfect within itself. As Williams says in his poem "Wild Orchard," from *An Early Martyr* (1935):

> Among blue leaves
> the apples green and red
> upon one tree stand out
> most enshrined.

> Still, ripe, heavy,
> spherical and close,
> they mark the hillside.
> It is a formal grandeur,
>
> a stateliness,
> a signal of finality
> and perfect ease.
> Among the savage
>
> aristocracy of rocks
> one, risen as a tree,
> has turned
> from his repose.[6]

Surely this is an instance of what Zukofsky would call the "totality of perfect rest." Nearly every figure in this poem signifies completion and self-sufficiency: the perpetual immediacy of natural processes completely subordinates the historical consciousness, even appropriating its linguistic authority, as in the phrase "the savage // aristocracy of rocks." And yet these lines appear in one of Williams's most embattled volumes from the heart of the Depression, a book in which Williams, as Robert Von Hallberg observes, "was trying . . . to reconcile the political demands of a disruptive decade with the kinds of descriptive and often delicate poetry he was then accustomed to writing."[7] Nor do the continued economic and political crises of American capitalism let the Objectivists ever rest:

> Now in the helicopters the casual will
> Is atrocious
>
> Insanity in high places,
> If it is true we must do these things
> We must cut our throats[8]

So says Oppen, at the height of the Vietnam War in *Of Being Numerous.* Here the world is far from perfect, and the poet is moved to speak from a profoundly subjective point of view, in the hope that his beliefs coincide with some measure of historical truth.

The means by which the Objectivists continually reformulate their ideals in the presence of historical necessities is thus an important gauge of poetry's continual attempt to create the Beautiful out of the Real. In his attack on what we may take to be the traditional "aura" of lyric poetry, Williams declares in *Spring and All* that " 'beauty' is not related to 'loveliness' but to a state in which reality plays a part."[9] It is therefore the responsibility of the poet to hold to the Real, despite the risk that his perceptions in themselves may alter, even distort, that with which he is confronted. It is for this reason that both Zukofsky and Oppen stress the notion of *sincerity*. Poetic utterance arises when consciousness is *moved* into language. As Zukofsky says in *An Objective* (1930): "In sincerity shapes appear concomitants of word combinations, precursors of (if there is continuance) completed sound or structure, melody or form."[10] But Zukofsky quickly adds that "presented with sincerity, the mind even tends to supply, in further suggestion, which does not attain rested totality, the totality not always found in sincerity and necessary only for perfect rest, complete appreciation."[11] Sincerity, to find a language for what is, enters into a fruitful tension with perfection, to achieve a language which completely fulfills itself. The result is a "rested totality," "objectification," "the apprehension satisfied completely as to the appearance of the art form as an object." The poem, then, is never complete until it articulates, in both form and content, the poet's simultaneous desires for sincerity and perfection.[12]

There is, of course, no assurance that any poem, once composed, has attained such a state. Poetry is not science; nor, in the end, are there purely empirical means of judging poetic accomplishment, however much the Objectivists longed to align literature with scientific principles. The crucial entrance of the term "perfection" in Zukofsky's equations should in itself indicate how much the Objectivists' project is concerned not only with that which is, but with that which longs to come into being. One may consider, in this regard, Williams's lifelong obsession with spring, the eternal return of all that has not yet been born. Likewise, Oppen's poetry continually returns to the theme of generation, both in terms of natural growth and historical succession. As he says of his task in *Of Being Numerous,*

> Because the known and the unknown
> Touch,
>
> One witnesses—.
> It is ennobling
> If one thinks so.[13]

Here Oppen refers to the unknown, "the metaphysical sense / Of the future." By a dialectical turn we may now see that for the Objectivists at their most advanced position, the plenitude of immediate experience is void if it lacks a vision of futurity that is both the complement and antithesis of their conventionally assumed philosophical position. As Zukofsky tells us in "A"-9, "Not today but tomorrow is their focus."

Yet Objectivist composition does resemble the scientific method in the emphasis placed on experimentation—that is, the *test of poetry*. Both

Zukofsky and Oppen refer to the idea of the poem as test. Zukofsky, in his evaluative anthology, refers primarily to form, but Oppen directs the idea back towards questions of cognition and belief:

> If no one were going to challenge me, I would say, "a test of truth." If I had to back it up I'd say anyway, "a test of sincerity"—that there is a moment, an actual time, when you believe something to be true, and you construct a meaning from these moments of conviction.[14]

In constructing a meaning—that is, a poem—from moments of conviction, the poet places himself in the open, at risk. The poem must provide the mediation between immediate perception and intuition, even when these two modes of cognition appear in conflict. One of Charles Olson's important contributions to Objectivist poetics centers on just this point. As he says in *Projective Verse* (1950):

> The objects which occur at every given moment of composition (of recognition, we can call it) are, can be, must be treated exactly as they do occur therein and not by any ideas or preconceptions from outside the poem, must be handled as a series of objects in field in such a way that a series of tensions (which they also are) are made to *hold*, and to hold exactly inside the content and context of the poem which has forced itself, through the poet and them, into being.[15]

Olson's concept of composition by field also implies a test of poetry, for he insists that ideas themselves, as they arise in the poem, must arise by virtue of the act of composition itself, and not through the application of any preconceptions. Beliefs must be intrinsic to the poem, and can, in a sense, be considered objects—as much as red wheelbarrows, saw horses, or deer in the forest. In the integrity of form, in the self-discoveries of language within the poem, all of the poet's "objects" are justified and made lawful. The Objectivist poem is thus the formal manifestation of a test of perceptions, ideas and beliefs—the result of a tension between sincerity and perfection. The poem as a rested totality depends upon the particular balance it achieves between the acknowledged state of immediate existence and the desired state of unfolding futurity.

But what is the historical and ideological significance of the operations of sincerity and perfection as they make manifest the rested totality of the Objectivist poem? As I have implied, it devolves upon the Objectivists to be the spokesmen, however unlikely, for a poetic tradition that speaks of reality while maintaining its utopian propensity. Bloch, in speaking of utopian consciousness, says that "it is *rectified*—but never refuted by the mere power of that which, at any particular time, *is*."[16] For the Objectivists, the achievement of sincerity within the poem demands constant "rectification," especially if one considers the political and social climate of the United States from the thirties to the sixties, when these poets were most active. In the following lines from Zukofsky's "A Song For the Year's End" (1944), the poet addresses just this issue:

> Then I shall go and write of my country,
> Have a job all my life
> Seldom write with grace again, be part of the world,
> See every man in forced labor,
> Dawn only where suburbs are *restricted*
> To people who take trains every morning,
> Never the gentleness that can be,
> The hope of the common man, the eyes that love leaves
> Any shade, thought or thing that makes all man uncommon[17]

Seldom write with grace again. One aspect of the tradition's utopian propensity may be that poets always recognize the necessity to rectify their desire for perfection in the face of "the mere power of that which, at any particular time, *is*." In Zukofsky's case, the necessity to bear witness, "be part of the world" for all its potentially crippling restrictions, forces him to admit the possibility that grace or beauty, as he has understood these qualities, must be sacrificed in the poet's direct encounter with historical truth. Sincerity here seems to take priority over the achievement of perfection, despite the fact that Zukofsky identified the totality of perfect rest as the ultimate goal of all poetry. Like his friend Williams (who was strongly influenced by Keats), Zukofsky is led inevitably back to the dialectic of Beauty and Truth, as the poet is compelled to test his desire for perfection against what Georg Lukács sternly calls "the sterile power of the merely existent."[18] It is in the Objectivists' act of testing—that is, writing the poem—that they may be seen as inheritors of the tradition I have described. Not only does Pound's privileging of the "poem including history" inspire much of their activity, but the necessity for what Oppen would later call "reportage" compels the Objectivists to hold to the contours of lived experience in ways that even a poet of the stature of Wallace Stevens does not. It is no accident that these poets provide an understanding of modern history, which, even if not couched in explicitly political terms, always emphasizes the relationship between the individual and society. "These were our times," writes Oppen, in one of the first poems after his famous thirty-year hiatus. The line could serve as an epigraph to the entire Objectivist endeavor.

It is with the historical intent and internal dynamics of Objectivist poetry in mind that we can briefly test two diverse poems by authors closest to the center of this tradition: Zukofsky's *"A"-9* and Oppen's *Of Being Numerous*. Formally speaking, it is difficult to imagine two more different modern poems. *"A"-9* is an elaborately rhymed double canzone, partly inspired by Pound's obsession with Cavalcanti's *Donna mi priegha* and incorporating Marx's economic theory, Spinoza's philsophy and Herbert Stanley Allen's introduction to atomic physics.[19] The poem is self-consciously abstract, implying, in its formidable syntax and over-determined themes, that it is meant for an audience of cognoscenti, as was Cavalcanti's canzone on love. It seems almost perverse to compare it with *Of Being Numerous,* the form of which argues against any sense of closure (especially the closure of rhyme) as it moves by leaps and associations of thought from one to another of its forty freely constructed and at times even prosaic sections. Its difficulty is thus of an entirely different order than that of Zukofsky's poem. Furthermore, because Oppen's poem is essentially a meditation on "the shipwreck/Of the singular," the estrangement of the intellectual from the masses and the resultant loss of community and praxis, the language, tortured as it is, attempts to speak directly and with clarity to as many readers as possible.

Yet both poems are tests in the manner adumbrated above. Beyond their differences in formal strategy, they share a common premise: that poetry, if it is to be of historical moment, must address itself to ideas that are central to its time; that poetry despite all ideological vicissitudes, can have as its object a kind of truth which, emerging intrinsically from the text, stands forth as the totalizing result of the human struggle for knowledge. What Zukofsky says of the objects of love applies equally to the object of these poems:

> Time does not move us, we are and love, searing
> Remembrance—veering from guises which cloak us,
> So defined as eternal, men invoke us.[20]

It remains to be seen how these poems achieve that state of rested totality that is the sine qua non of Objectivism. This is perhaps more easily seen in the case of *"A"-9.* The poem is a fine balance between the notions of sincerity and perfection, as expressed in the form of the complementary canzones on labor and love, economic necessity and moral freedom. We read the poem to experience sensually the manner in which such ideas move dialectically in relation to material conditions, for this is precisely what the rhyme scheme and dense syntax offer us in linguistic and musical terms. Consider these lines from the third strophe of the first canzone:

> Hands, heart, not value made us, and of any
> Desired perfection the projection solely,
> Lives worked us slowly to delight the senses,
> Of their fire shall you find us, of the many
> Acts of direction, not defection . . .[21]

Anyone who has read *Capital* Volume I remembers the high comedy of its opening chapters, in which Marx develops the concepts of labor and exchange value and commodity fetishism. Zukofsky's verse transforms the truth content of Marx's work into a highly refined music; the sincerity of the poet's political beliefs is tempered by the perfection of the achieved form. The achievement of perfect form *is* the test of sincerity: as Zukofsky says at the poem's conclusion,

> . . . rhyme now how song's exaction
> Is your distraction—related is equated,
> How else is love's distance approximated.[22]

In its use of free verse, *Of Being Numerous* is a more typical Objectivist poem, but form plays as significant a part in determining its totality as it does in "A"-9. As a long series poem, Oppen's masterpiece offers a succession of variously linked moments, the shape of each conforming to the poet's exactingly measured thought as he broods over his theme. If in "A"-9 form signifies the desire for perfection, in *Of Being Numerous* form always adheres to sincerity in the utterance. Note the carefully articulated lines of section 6:

> We are pressed, pressed on each other,
> We will be told at once
> Of anything that happens
> And the discovery of fact bursts
> In a paroxysm of emotion
> Now as always. Crusoe
>
> We say was
> 'Rescued'.
> So we have chosen.[23]

Even as rhyme in Zukofsky's poem creates a sense of self-sustained perfection, line breaks here indicate sincerely observed belief. The first long line repeats "pressed" in such a way as to convey the physical sensation; the fourth line, with "bursts" as its last word, moves us from "the discovery of facts"·to "a paroxysm of emotion"—precisely the thematic movement of the poem in its totality. The reference to Crusoe, recalling not only Defoe's novel but Marx's ironic use of it in *Capital,* suggests the impossibility of the singular life, as well as the loss of self when such a life is brought back into contact with the world at large. The poem moves naturally then to section 7, its most direct statement of theme:

> Obsessed, bewildered

> By the shipwreck
> Of the singular
>
> We have chosen the meaning
> Of being numerous[24]

In short, Oppen's successive recognitions of belief propel the poem forward, with each section achieving its full meaning from what comes before and what follows it. The poem comes to rest only through such movement; perfection suggests itself not in completion but openness: "Children and the grass / In the wind and the voices of men and women // To be carried about the sun forever."[25]

The major works of Oppen and Zukofsky (as well as Williams in such poems as *Asphodel, That Greeny Flower*) often resolve themselves in images of light, air, even music: phenomena that approach and serve as tropes for an invisible world of pure presence—what Oppen, in one of his late poems, calls the "Hidden starry life." And indeed, it seems inevitable that this poetry, which arose partly from a desire for immediate contact with the material world, should eventually articulate not a transcendent vision, but a vision of immanence, of material plenitude so inexhaustible that it seems to spill over the boundaries of discrete material forms.[26] Beginning *"A"-23* (the last purely linguistic movement of the poem, before Zukofsky allows it to merge into Celia's *L. Z. Masque*), the poet sings of

> An unforeseen delight a round
> beginning ardent; to end blest
> presence less than nothing thrives:
> a world worn in whose
> happiest reins preempt their histories
> which cannot help or hurt
> a foreseen curve where many
> loci would dispose and *and's*
> compound creature and creature together.[27]

The extraordinarily condensed syntax is itself a sign of the matter of the verse at this point: in a world of "blest / presence," histories are preempted and all is joined together in a single great sentence, in which "*and's* / compound creature and creature together."[28]

We usually do not think of the Objectivists as visionary poets, but such a term may be applied to them with complete validity. In his study of American visionary poetry, Hyatt H. Waggoner asserts that

the visionary poet neither imagines the values he celebrates nor believes them into being but attentively and creatively perceives, discovers, or uncovers them. So they are finally not his but the world's, existing with or without his awareness of them.[29]

Such a statement complements the Objectivists' own theories, in that the poet's work is meant to be a recording, a report, or a test of the conditions found to be preexisting in the world. The accurate report, the test of sincerity, may become a vision—not in the sense of an ephemeral ideal, but of a thing seen, perceived, believed. Objectivist poetry depends upon such acts of faith regardless of its particular content; hence its astonishing range of subjects, from the most simple natural phenomena to the most complex human ideas and institutions. In this sense, it may not be too far-fetched to consider that Objectivism finally restores the aura to modern poetry, an aura not based on ritualized distance, but on what Oppen calls "a substantial language / Of clarity, and of respect."

But if all that I have said is true of Objectivism, is the term itself finally a misnomer? I do not believe so; the renewed emphasis these poets place upon objective phenomena, despite, as we have seen, their own occasional reluctance to endorse such a source of æsthetic value wholeheartedly, indicates the importance of the "merely existent" to recent American poetry generally. Thus if we leave this poetry with a sense of its traditional grounding, we must also depart with an appreciation for the wealth of its historically appropriate inventiveness. The strategies of the Objectivists—I hesitate now to speak of them as an ideology—are essential to the task of continually reorienting the tradition to worldly conditions that demand fully sustained poetic utterance. Despite the obvious difficulties of such a poetry, we are convinced of Oppen's sincerity when he exclaims

Clarity, clarity, surely clarity is the most beautiful thing in the world,
A limited, limiting clarity[30]

This is surely a "subjective" statement. But Robert Creeley, perhaps the last direct heir of the Objectivists, settles that question too, in a little essay called "A Note on the Objective" (1951):

However right it may be to damn the use of the *subjective* method as an excuse for emotional claptrap, it's apt to push us away from any understanding of the *subjective* in a more basic character, i.e., "belonging to, or of, or due to, the consciousness . . ." Impossible to write anything, lacking this relation of its content to oneself. Put another way: things have to come in before they can go out.

Perhaps best to junk both terms, or at least to understand this necessary balance, one with the other. We can't stand outside our content and at the same time we can't eat it like an apple, etc. And

perhaps, finally, more to the point than either of these two stances is
that one which maintains: a man and his objects must both be pres-
ences in this field of force we call a poem.[31]

Creeley's conclusion, his righting of the balance, is the result of the
Objectivists' long struggle with these most basic poetic terms.

O'Hara, Ashbery, and the Loss of the Sublime

Farewell to an idea . . . The cancellings,
The negations are never final. The father sits
In space, wherever he sits, of bleak regard,

As one that is strong in the bushes of his eyes.
He says no to no and yes to yes. He says yes
to no; and in saying yes he says farewell.
                                   —Wallace Stevens,
                                   "The Auroras of Autumn"

The aesthetic and ideological implications of the Objectivists' privileg-
ing of immediacy, and their radical valuation of the plenitude of
momentary, material existence, in some ways arrive at their logical con-
clusions in the poetry of Frank O'Hara and John Ashbery.[1] The promise
of perfection in futurity, apparently so unlikely in Williams, Zukofsky,
Oppen, would seem almost nonexistent in the work of these more recent
poets. Yet as we have observed, it is only through the dialectical tensions
of sincerity and perfection, or necessity and freedom, that the Objec-
tivists create poetry of historical moment; and I will argue that similar
tensions prevail in O'Hara's and Ashbery's work. I am aware, of course,
that these poets are viewed ordinarily as practitioners of a mode of
studied casualness, whose appropriation of quotidian detail signifies
their adherence to an ideology of detachment and ironic play, in which
all scales of moral and aesthetic values are leveled or flattened, and
naturally, any manner of traditional poetic transcendence is rejected. As
Charles Molesworth, one of the most perceptive critics of these poets,
has said of O'Hara:

Central to O'Hara's poetics is the absence of any idealizing impulse, or
any clash of opposing values; all is levelled into an ever more inclusive
'yea,' and the meretricious mixes easily with the meritorious.[2]

The same could well be said of Ashbery.

Likewise, history in the work of these poets is regarded at best as some great attic to be ransacked for objects in the poem; any serious encounter with the past as a meaningful structural component of the present is liable to be attacked as nostalgia. "Time farted," jokes Ashbery, in one of his many parodies of rancid Romanticism. But the joke may prove to be at the author's expense, despite the critics' descriptions of O'Hara's and Ashbery's strategies for dissolving time into the now and nothing more— the now, that is, of empty, homogeneous time.[3] Temporal and spatial immediacy remain impossibilities in the poem, whether sought under the aegis of Objectivism, "Personism" or the free play of language (cour-tesy of Stevens or Apollinaire). The poem is marked by literary and social history; indeed, its existence as a text is constituted by such forces, regardless of its self-referential appearance.

The leveling process that takes place in the work of these poets is a search for historicity, an unevenly weighted dialectical struggle to articu-late a notion of the sublime, which must ultimately be viewed as an absence, impossible to cast off or forget. Ashbery himself seems partially aware of this in those famous lines from "The Skaters":

> . . . the carnivorous
> Way of these lines is to devour their own nature leaving
> Nothing but a bitter impression of absence, which as we know
>   involves presence, but still,
> Nevertheless these are fundamental absences, struggling to get up
>   and be off with themselves.[4]

The quiet terror adumbrated here brings me to what I consider the best modern definition of the sublime, which is Kenneth Burke's. Appropri-ately enough for our discussion of two of the funniest of recent poets, Burke contrasts the sublime with the ridiculous:

> As soon as we approach the subject in these terms, we have in the very terms themselves a constant reminder that the *threat* is the basis of beauty. Some vastness of magnitude, power, or distance, dispropor-tionate to ourselves, is "sublime." We recognize it with awe. We find it dangerous in its fascination. And we equip ourselves to confront it by piety, by stylistic medicine, and by structural assertion (form, a public matter that symbolically enrolls us with allies who will share the bur-dens with us). The ridiculous, on the contrary, equips us by impiety, as we refuse to allow the threat [of] its authority: we rebel, and coura-geously play pranks when "acts of God" themselves are oppressing us . . .[5]

Many of the finest poems by both poets arise from the dynamic conflict between the sublime and the ridiculous as Burke defines them. For two poets as steeped in tradition as O'Hara and Ashbery, identification with the sublime, fascination with the plenitude of experience perceived as an other, is threatening both in its presence *and* absence. Thus, in reading these poets, we encounter again and again passages that elevate us through their yearning diction and passionate rhetorical gestures, only to find them ironically deflated or dismissed by ambivalence.

The loss of the sublime in O'Hara and Ashbery is contingent upon these poets' ambivalence toward the sublime itself. Because they have not altogether rejected the high idealism of the Romantic lyric (and in this regard they are less radical than the Objectivists), but forever doubt its power of assertion, theirs is a poetry built on vacillation and the play of extremes. Paradoxically, the linguistic manifestation of such movement is the leveled world of the poems, the flat surfaces so often found in Ashbery, the self-satisfied jumble of incongruities in O'Hara. At worst, both poets seem to endlessly imitate themselves, and despite the Postmodern temptation to read the bodies of their work as ongoing acts of *écriture,* I would argue that they must be evaluated with a carefully selective eye. It is also extremely tempting to see them, along with their epigones, as Molesworth does—comprising a mode of poetic discourse that coincides with the conditions that late capitalism imposes upon art, in which expressions of alienation, ambivalence and sheer banality are made willingly by the artists into marketable productions.[6] Gerald Graff's discussion of capitalist ideology as based upon the fluid commodity form would bear out such an analysis, since "the culture of capitalism is a culture of perpetual metamorphosis," and the poetry of the New York School is nothing if not in perpetual metamorphosis.[7] And indeed, I must agree that a great deal of the pervasive influence this poetry has had must be due to just such factors.

I would maintain, however, that O'Hara's and Ashbery's best poems contain the expression of a highly significant moment in contemporary poetic history. Although these poets never really challenge bourgeois modes of discourse and cognition (often they actually reify them), and rarely, and never willingly attain to a level of prophetic utterance,[8] they imply and sometimes openly declare that a vision of or even a desire for perfection has been stifled in them. On the one hand, these poets feel, like the Objectivists before them, that they must remain faithful to the empirical conditions of American reality, celebrating the immediate and quotidian in their ruthless demands for truthful attention and expression. Hence theirs is a poetry of process that often fits the contours of contemporary consciousness with compelling, if not distressing accuracy. On the other hand, O'Hara and Ashbery are always aware of the omnipresent "reasoning of the eternal voices" (the phrase is from O'Hara's "To the Harbormaster"), the lure of a language and a worldview—a tradition—that in themselves have become a threatening other. Harold Bloom is correct in naming Ashbery a belated poet who treats transcendental experience with "detachment with respect," though he does not consider the ideological implications of this condition.[9] For both Ashbery and O'Hara, tradition as a source of transcendental meaning and value has been called into doubt, though they recognize it to be the primary source of their extraordinary poetic aptitudes. Thus they must take the massive risk of subverting traditional poetic strategies and values with regard to the sublime because they sense that they have been victimized by history, or to use Burke's ironic term, "acts of God." As O'Hara says:

> It may be that poetry makes life's nebulous events tangible to me and restores their detail; or conversely, that poetry brings forth the intangible quality of incidents which are all too concrete and circumstantial. Or each on specific occasions, or both all the time.[10]

Difficult as it may be, given the fine capacity for amusement we find in both poets, we must recognize the potential for tragedy in this statement. As in Ashbery's beautiful poem "As One Put Drunk into the Packet-Boat," "a sigh heaves from all the small things on earth," for poetry can never sufficiently bring forth the intangible quality of which O'Hara speaks—at least not for these poets. We are again reminded of Walter Benjamin's concept of the aura, for under capitalism, the objects of the material world, transformed into commodities, both lose their sensuous individuality and, through a loss of ritualized distance, impose their mere concreteness too strongly on the perceiver. O'Hara's and Ashbery's poems often attempt to recover a lost balance between the immediacy of exterior events and the interior world of personal values, the tangible and the intangible, which would in turn provide access to a renewed experience of the sublime. Instead they find

> The books, the papers, the old garters and union-suit buttons
> Kept in a white cardboard box somewhere, and all the lower
> Versions of cities flattened under the equalizing night[11]

—the night, as Hegel would say, in which all cows are black. Capitulating to those conditions which flatten Ashbery's cities (no doubt the same lacustrine cities of his earlier poem), the poet finds himself celebrating the night in spite of himself, believing that it "gives more than it takes." One must be drunk indeed to believe so, but this explains the alternating moods of exultation and resignation we find throughout the poems. When the sublime is approached, as when Ashbery thinks "The great, formal affair was beginning, orchestrated, / Its colors concentrated in a glance, a ballade / That takes in the whole world," he is invariably informed (or informs himself) that "You have slept in the sun / Longer than the sphinx, and are none the wiser for it."

So the loss of the sublime is a loss of wisdom as well, and despite the sweet consoling power of this poetry, as witnessed, for example, by the many reviewers who felt a personal allure in reading "Self-Portrait in a Convex Mirror,"[12] consciousness remains illuminated from within, as the poems talk incessantly to and about themselves. Some would argue that poetry since the Romantics has been nothing but a long exercise in solipsism, which may be why Ashbery and O'Hara seem at times to be the end of a particular line,[13] and also to be so open to the mere reflection of a current aesthetic ideology. Ashbery has discussed the ideological implications of his work, comparing it to more overtly political poetry ("a poem which is in effect a sermon") and citing Auden's "poetry makes nothing happen." Yet during the Vietnam conflict, he participated in anti-war poetry readings. As he explains:

> I did this somewhat dubiously because I felt that poetry makes nothing happen, nevertheless, here was a case where I felt that even though this is true, maybe people will, by the nature of my non-political poetry, be persuaded to become more *people*. I mean a person will become more of a person and will therefore do these not only politically helpful and constructive things, but things that will make him more aware of his own life and the people around him and will influence his actions on a number of levels, not just one.[14]

The irony here, as I see it, is that poetry like Ashbery's, while perhaps making one more aware of one's life, does not offer any means to determine the priorities in one's life. If poetry is to be of continued worth, then it must in some ways be a means to greater cognitive powers, schooling human thought and feeling to allow for the continuance of creativity. "This is what we are" must be translatable into "this is what we might be." By self-consciously calling such a translation into doubt, the poems of Ashbery and O'Hara enshrine the historical impasse of which they are both creators and creations. Like Stevens in *Notes toward a Supreme Fiction*, they can only declare "I have not but I am and as I am, I am." But whereas in Stevens, or even more so, in William Bronk, such a statement is rendered historically appropriate through the sheer rigor of syntax and the radical purity of diction, when such ideas are approached in O'Hara or Ashbery, the result is an appalling loss of vision and at times of linguistic integrity. And it is just this integrity of utterance for which these poets yearn, though it cannot be attained without simultaneously arriving at a positive ground of historicity.

If Ashbery and O'Hara are poets of process, of "indeterminacy" and open form, they are so in spite of their deepest inclinations; and in this regard, their work can be seen as a negation of the negation, which endures and finds its voice in its self-conscious insufficiency. As O'Hara says in these crucial lines from "Hotel Transylvanie":

> yet you will always live in a jealous society of accident
> you will never know how beautiful you are or how beautiful
> the other is, you will continue to refuse to die for yourself
> you will continue to sing on trying to cheer everyone up
> and they will know as they listen with excessive pleasure that you're
>   dead
>   and they will not mind that they have let you entertain
> at the expense of the only thing you want in the world[15]

What makes these lines so pathetic and yet so powerful is the haunting way in which O'Hara speaks to himself, for he knows but refuses to acknowledge his desire to be a poet of the sublime. His willingness to assume the role of a mere entertainer conflicts with the potential for beauty he feels within himself, and the result is a kind of eloquent hysteria.[16] Because he knows this to be the case, the poem becomes a "sublime moment of dishonest hope," the moment when the gambler in the casino must accept himself for what he is, with no illusions:

> . . . you have only to be
> as you are being, as you must be, as you always are, as you shall be
>   forever
> no matter what fate deals you or the imagination discards like a
>   tyrant
> as the drums descend and summon the hatchet over the tinselled
>   realities

Fate deals the cards, and win or lose, the game must be played, the lover must love, the poem must be written. The terrible sense of a life out of hand, of a discourse beyond control (a similar but even stronger feeling pervades the last poems of Jack Spicer) drives the text forward despite itself, until the final tropes of suicide and obscurity seem the only ones strong enough to express the metaphysical loss. Something has gone wrong here, the stakes were too high: the past forecloses on the self-indulgent present, the hatchet is summoned over the "tinselled realities," and the future, towards which the sublime looks for the resolution of its agon, is eradicated: "for if the floods of tears arrive they will wash it all away."

Both "As One Put Drunk into the Packet-Boat" and "Hotel Transylvanie" enact a ritual of renunciation, a celebration of loss, in which the existential possibility for meaningful human action is cast into doubt and the metaphysical sense of the future, to again borrow Oppen's phrase, is deliberately extinguished. The gestures of sublime poetry, particularly those of Romanticism, are put to use in such a way as to preclude the chance of genuinely sublime emotions from taking hold of the utterance. Rather than face vast power (fate, nature or most threatening of all, history) with "structural assertion," these poets rely on diffident limpidity (Ashbery) or melodramatic collapse (O'Hara) to avoid the confrontation. In comparing them, a number of critics have distinguished Ashbery's greater detachment from O'Hara's more engaged and personal style, and I think this distinction holds for "Packet-Boat" and "Hotel Transylvanie," as well as for the poets' works in general.[17] I would also argue that Ashbery's most important poems are based on a kind of discourse that at least gives the appearance of syntactic coherence, regardless of its rhetorical flourishes, while O'Hara's best poems frequently employ syntactic disjunctures and fragmentation that are of strategic importance to their total effect. But *lost authority* remains, paradoxically enough, the commanding impulse in this poetic endeavor. The absence of the sublime may offer relief to many "radical" Postmodernists, who perceive the sublime as nothing more than an exhausted mode of bourgeois literary discourse, but its absence provides a devastating tension for these poets who experience it first-hand. Let us consider the case in some few more of their poems.

A strong case might be made for O'Hara as "quintessentially a poet of the domestic and the quotidian"[18] to quote Charles Altieri. Such a case would focus on O'Hara's "I do this I do that" poems, like the justly famous "The Day Lady Died" (which for my purposes is an exception that proves the rule), indicating the extent to which aesthetic and social values are renewed through the poet's engagement with the personal, spontaneous and fluid matter of his poems. An analysis of these "lunch hour poems" leads James Breslin to conclude that O'Hara "moves through a demystified and secular world of immediacy, from which all vertical, transcendent extensions of meaning have disappeared."[19] This seems to me little more than a reification of those conditions against which O'Hara struggled, and the "I do this I do that" poems, lovely as some of them are, strike me as an attempt to find solace in lesser pleasures when the struggle for the historicity of the sublime proves overwhelming. A brief glance at the table of contents of the *Collected Poems* shows us the way O'Hara vacillates between these two kinds of poems. Indeed, Breslin argues that "O'Hara was never seduced by style in the first place; instead, he gives us a multiplicity of styles."[20] While some would claim this as an indication of his range, flexibility and dedication to a poetry of process, I would take such a condition as evidence for his approaches to and retreats from the sublime, which he makes throughout his tragically short but remarkably productive career.

Keeping O'Hara's better-known and influential poems of immediacy in mind, we turn to a relatively early piece, "The Hunter," one of his most overt appropriations of the Romantic mode. Far from being a parody (as is sometimes the case with both him and Ashbery), this is a poem of the utmost seriousness and a relatively high degree of traditional decorum. The first stanza openly gestures toward the Romantic sublime, while hinting at the ridiculous:

> He set out and kept hunting
> and hunting. Where, he thought
> and thought, is the real chamois?
> and can I kill it where it is?
> He had brought with him only a dish
> of pears. The autumn wind soared
> above the trails where the drops
> of the chamois led him further.
> The leaves dropped around him
> like pie-plates. The stars fell
> one by one into his eyes and burnt.[21]

The hunter, setting out on his deadly heroic quest, bearing the absurdly domestic dish of pears, is doomed to meet the humiliation he will encounter by the poem's end.[22] Nature is a fateful antagonist, but seems to mock the hunter as well. There is no question that he is a chosen figure, as the stars fall into his eyes and burn, and later, in the midst of his struggle, manna falls. But to be chosen in this case means to be victimized, as the last part of the poem amply demonstrates:

> He saw the world below him, brilliant
> as a floor, and steaming with gold,
> with distance. There were occasionally
> rifts in the cloud where the face
> of a woman appeared, frowning. He
> had gone higher. He wore ermine.
> He thought, why did I come? and then,
> I have come to rule! The chamois came.
>
> The chamois found him and they came
> in droves to humiliate him. Alone,
> in the clouds, he has humiliated.

Straightforward and bitter, O'Hara concentrates a number of traditional figures into these fast-moving lines. Looking down from the heights of vision, the hunter sees the world as a promised kingdom, as he is about to be transformed into a prophet, king or deity. But Ananke, the goddess of fate, who is also a disapproving muse, forbids such transcendence. The chamois appear, the original objects of the hunter's quest to subdue nature, and the hunter is apparently paralyzed. They refuse to grant him his rightful inheritance; he has been led on his quest as if he were the butt of an immense cosmic joke. Unable to fulfill his destiny, he is made to appear ridiculous, and any chance to redeem himself through traditional heroic action is denied.

Clearly, the Romantic quest poem is an insufficient mode of expression here—not, as one would usually think, because it is "outdated," but because the emotions ordinarily associated with the poet/quester are turned back upon themselves and are made to reveal the inadequacy of the quest itself. The chamois (nature) and the woman in the cloud (fate) are both, as Yeats would call them, "self-born mockers of man's enterprise," but rather than offer a vision of unity of being as in "Among School Children," they simply allow the hunter to delude himself and then humiliate him. The same inability to achieve unity of being may be found in the plaintive "To the Harbormaster," which lacks explicitly Romantic trappings. In this poem the mysterious, paternalistic harbormaster may be read as another figure of remote, transcendental power, whom O'Hara is compelled to address:

> . . . To
> you I offer my hull and the tattered cordage
> of my will. The terrible channels where
> the wind drives me against the brown lips
> of the reeds are not all behind me. Yet
> I trust the sanity of my vessel; and
> if it sinks, it may well be in answer
> to the reasoning of the eternal voices,
> the waves which have kept me from reaching you.[23]

The poet's attempt to achieve the sublime is frustrated by the sublime powers themselves, though it is they who urge him on. Like the father who encourages his son and yet denies him, the harbormaster is perfectly content to watch the poet sink, defeated by the limits of nature and the self, knowing that he will be celebrated in all his distance as the poet goes down.

Such disasters, however self-willed, lead O'Hara to question the sanity of his vessel, which he previously claimed to trust. The divided self and its implications for the modern sublime become the basic theme for what is now regarded as one of O'Hara's most important poems, "In Memory

of My Feelings," which in one sense, like a number of Ashbery's impor-
tant poems, issues directly from the closing lines of Stevens's "Esthétique
du Mal":

> And out of what one sees and hears and out
> Of what one feels, who could have thought to make
> So many selves, so many sensuous worlds,
> As if the air, the mid-day air, was swarming
> With the metaphysical changes that occur,
> Merely in living as and where we live.[24]

Stevens, in seeking to resolve the split between ethics and aesthetics in
his work, concludes that the myriad possibilities offered to the self in the
sensuous world can provide sufficient meaning when any transcendental
meaning has disappeared. His conclusion, however, is not completely
satisfying: "the metaphysical changes" linger on in "a physical world" due
to the conditional "As if." O'Hara inherits this problematic situation
when, instead of describing the condition of having many selves while
still speaking from a relatively unified self, he enacts this many-selved
condition.

"In Memory of My Feelings" has been considered an act of triumphant
renewal, in which the poet recognizes his essential self in all its multi-
plicity, and posits his potential for creative activity therein.[25] This is a
typically Postmodern idealization of the existential freedom of psycho-
logical processes. The poem's form is open and highly fragmented,
embracing numerous possibilities for the self. Its complex texture, shift-
ing grandly in tone and imagery, signifies the apparently endless meta-
morphoses in O'Hara's career as a latter-day "camelion Poet." What must
be recognized, however, is that O'Hara longs painfully for a unified self
as a means of ordering and evaluating the conditions of his life, though
he is usually able to mask such longing with his typical good humor.
Breslin is probably closer to the truth than most other critics when he
notes of "In Memory of My Feelings" that "the absence of a literal level
derives from O'Hara's inability, made clear at the end of the poem, to
reach any originating cause or source for his feelings, his 'selves'."[26] The
long catalogues of alternative identities, aggressively surrealistic or suf-
fused with dreamlike memories, betray an underlying urgency, a desire
to be encircled by the central self, the serpent who is both threatening
and hypnotically attractive. The famous phrase "Grace / to be born and
live as variously as possible" (part of which is inscribed on O'Hara's
tombstone!) immediately precedes the more negative "The conception /
of the masque barely suggests the sordid identifications," indicating,
through this juxtaposition, O'Hara's profound ambivalence toward a
poetry of merely lived experience. "Beneath these lives / the ardent lover

of history hides," declares the poet, but that lover is never able to emerge from the morass of existential options, none of which provide any real alternatives to the quotidian affairs of the self-absorbed life. O'Hara guiltily evades history through his synchronous verbal strategies, his leveled poetic mindscape, but when it is "the serpent's turn" at the end of the poem, he cannot avoid the confrontation:

> The hero, trying to unhitch his parachute,
> stumbles over me. It is our last embrace.
>   And yet
> I have forgotten my loves, and chiefly that one, the cancerous
> statue which my body could no longer contain,
>
>   against my will
>   against my love
> become art,
>   I could not change it into history
> and so remember it,
>   and I have lost what is always and everywhere
> present, the scene of my selves, the occasion of these ruses,
> which I myself and singly must now kill
>   and save the serpent in their midst.[27]

Unlike Jack Spicer, who really wished to eradicate the hero in order to allow for a poetry of "dictated" otherness, O'Hara remains enamored of the heroic stance, and he returns to the figure of the poet-hero throughout his career. If he believes this embrace to be their last one, it is only because he is in the process, which never concludes, of reconciling himself to the supposed unavailability of sublime expression. Likewise, he is "not quite" like the serpent, who is "coiled around the central figure, / the heart," while the poet is "the opposite of visionary." And indeed, the poem ends in what could be called an anti-vision. Against his will, against his love, O'Hara has transformed the multiplicity of his existence into art, but he realizes that "I could not change it into history." This is a fearsome admission for a poet to make: it implies a loss of textual authority which may be admirable in its selflessness but suicidal as a poetic stance. For a poet with O'Hara's ambition and background, there is no avoiding the "egotistical sublime," as Keats himself found out. Thus, he loses the unified scene of his many selves and ultimately cannot save the serpent. The poem becomes, as Alan Feldman says of O'Hara's work generally, "a confluence of feeling and perception that is suffused with a sense of its own passing away."[28]

O'Hara's poetry, then, is always charged with a feeling of lost potential, as an integral self that could endure the vicissitudes of daily life continually dissolves into multiple identities and momentary experiences. For O'Hara, as much as for Pound in the *Cantos*, "Time is the evil," because for both men, time as experienced in the exterior world is mere duration. But unlike Pound, O'Hara refuses to privilege any interior events or moments in history; in his world in which all value systems have been leveled and metamorphosis is the only constant, cessation, stasis, death are the greatest threats. O'Hara's most powerful outpouring against death is the thundering "Ode to Joy." The poem celebrates the moment of sexual climax as that one point in time when past and future collapse into the present and death is thwarted. In a rhetorical tour de force, O'Hara attempts to remake civilization into an image of personal ecstasy:

> Buildings will go up into the dizzy air as love itself goes in
>   and up the reeling life that it has chosen for once or all
> while in the sky a feeling of intemperate fondness will excite the
>   birds
>   to swoop and veer like flies crawling across absorbed limbs
> that weep a pearly perspiration on the sheets of brief attention
> and the hairs dry out that summon anxious declarations of the
>   organs
>   as they rise like buildings to the needs of temporary neighbors
>   pouring hunger through the heart to feed desire in intravenous
>   ways
> like the ways of gods with humans in the innocent combinations of
>   light
> and flesh or as the legends ride their heroes through the dark to
>   found
> great cities where all life is possible to maintain as long as time
>   which wants us to remain for cocktails in a bar and after dinner
>   lets us live with it
> No more dying[29]

This is one of the few genuinely utopian passages in O'Hara's work: by suggesting the possibility of an eternally orgasmic present, the poet radically de-historicizes the work of civilization, which appears spontaneously in an unmediated instant of desire. The surging images create a metamorphic landscape of the city and the body; the insistent rhythms provide a sense of totality that is rarely found in O'Hara's work. O'Hara is almost scandalously direct: "No more dying," as if art were no longer a sublimation of libidinal energy, but the voice of that energy itself. Freud, in *Civilization and Its Discontents,* makes an observation that seems to criticize and endorse O'Hara's strategy simultaneously:

> So, also, the two urges, the one towards personal happiness and the other towards union with other human beings, must struggle with each other in every individual; and so, also, the two processes of individual and of cultural development must stand in hostile opposi-

tion to each other and mutually dispute the ground. But this struggle between the individual and society is not a derivative of the contradiction—probably an irreconcilable one—between the primal instincts of Eros and death. It is a dispute within the economics of the libido, comparable to the contest concerning the distribution of libido between ego and objects; and it does admit of an eventual accommodation of the individual, as, it may be hoped, it will also do in the future of civilization, however much that civilization may oppress the life of the individual today.[30]

O'Hara apparently bypasses the "hostile opposition" between personal satisfaction and the work of civilization, and thus from the perspective of the present, again evades the necessity of historically imposed libidinal sublimation. At the same time, however, he anticipates that utopian future when the "economics of the libido" will "admit of an eventual accommodation of the individual." The poem becomes the immediate articulation of erotic, utopian plenitude, an ode to joy which is seemingly unhindered by historical necessity. And in that such tension is lacking in its utterance, it is, as it were, a sublime evasion of the sublime. This is the furthest point in O'Hara's poetic development, when the dialectic of sublime absence and presence, the search for historicity, is cancelled, and loss becomes joy.

If O'Hara's poetry reaches its extreme through its evasions of the sublime, we may say that Ashbery's poetry is entirely permeated with such gestures. Of course, a discussion of Ashbery's work in this context is less unusual than one of O'Hara's, since a number of recent critics have taken their cue from Harold Bloom, placing Ashbery in the tradition of visionary poetry in general and Romanticism in particular. Ashbery is the object of at least two competing critical models, as exemplified by Bloom on the one hand and Marjorie Perloff on the other. A schism of this sort is a sure sign of ideological contradiction: normative literary criticism cannot merely "describe" or even "analyze" Ashbery's work; its presence in itself politicizes and polarizes the literary establishment, and the guise of objective scrutiny is dropped in favor of partisanship and rear-guard action.[31] In such a climate—when confronted with a burgeoning Ashbery "industry"!—Fredric Jameson's advice in regard to "obscure" poetry is especially pertinent:

Thus, faced with obscure poetry, the naive reader attempts at once to *interpret*, to resolve the immediate difficulties back into the transparency of rational thought; whereas for a dialectically trained reader, it is the obscurity itself which is the object of his reading, and its specific quality and structure that which he attempts to define and to compare with other forms of verbal opacity. Thus our thought no longer takes official problems at face value; but walks behind the screen to assess the very origin of the subject-object relationship in the first place.[32]

Walking behind the screen created by the critics' relationship to Ashbery's work, we find the inherent contradiction of much recent criticism when it is called upon to make canonic evaluation of a novel and obscure text: the desire, on the one hand, to endorse the text as genuinely (Post)modern, a fashionable expression of contemporary reality (a distortion, one could say, of Pound's dictum "Make it new!"); the need, on the other hand, to recuperate the text in the service of a nostalgia for a false idealization of tradition (a sequence of "touchstones" or Oedipally empowered "strong poets"). In regard to Ashbery, the former view severs his actual relationship to the sublime, making him exclusively a poet of immediate process and self-reflexivity. The latter view reifies his relationship to the sublime, making him purely the visionary heir of post-Romantic hermeticism. Of Ashbery's recent commentators, the one who has most successfully managed to bypass this split is Alan Williamson, whose reading may be considered a more positive counterpart to mine. In his interpretation of "Definition of Blue," Williamson derives "the peculiar Ashberian justification (and, at the same time, transcendence) of the avant-garde. Endless self-consciousness makes every gesture the possible occasion for endless self-knowledge."[33] What Williamson sees as "Ashbery's remarkable refusal to relinquish either surface or depth" contributes to his view of the poet's "interior search for a lost paradise."[34]

But what Williamson regards as a search, even informed by a "social and historical intelligence,"[35] I cannot help viewing as less deliberate and purposeful movement. As I have indicated, Ashbery's importance may be measured in the way he is pulled between the poles of self-reflexive play and visionary intensity; and at times the prevailing tension in his work is manifested in a language that is maddeningly tempting in its ambivalence. And because ambivalence is not only the central emotion in Ashbery, but in most of his critics as well, it is no wonder he has become the figurehead (or perhaps the black hole) of the history of poetry in our time. Consider what he says in "Evening in the Country":

> Now as my questioning but admiring gaze expands
> To magnificent outposts, I am not so much at home
> With these memorabilia of vision as on a tour
> Of my remotest properties, and the eidolon
> Sinks into the effective "being" of each thing,
> Stump or shrub, and they carry me inside
> On motionless explorations of how dense a thing can be,

How light, and these are finished before they have begun
Leaving me refreshed and somehow younger.[36]

In such graceful but ill-fated lines as these, Ashbery could honestly be called the spokesman of a literary generation. Poetic effort is not an attempt to reach "magnificent outposts," but instead is merely a tour of that which has already been expropriated and turned into property, so that the poet may indulge in "motionless explorations"—of the self, of culture, of the immediate environment—that leave him "refreshed and somehow younger." This would be mere dilettantism except for the "memorabilia of vision" which even in their absence discomfit and threaten the poet. What has happened to Ashbery's memory of vision? To what most distant reaches of the pleasing country real estate has the sublime escaped?

There is no simple answer to these admittedly irreverent questions, for Ashbery approaches the sublime even more frequently than O'Hara throughout his career. But let us consider this brief lyric from *Some Trees* (more or less contemporary with O'Hara's "The Hunter"), entitled, appropriately enough, "The Hero":

> Whose face is this
> So stiff against the blue trees,
>
> Lifted to the future
> Because there is no end?
>
> But that has faded
> Like flowers, like the first days
>
> Of good conduct. Visit
> The strong man. Pinch him—
>
> There is no end to his
> Dislike, the accurate one.[37]

In its diction, syntax, stanza structure and rhythm, this poem bears the clear stamp of Wallace Stevens, as Harold Bloom would readily tell us. And indeed, "The Hero" swerves—but not only from Stevens's rhetorical influence, but from Stevens's own attenuated version of sublime heroism. Stevens's hero is the self-anointed god-king of "Tea at the Palaz of Hoon" or later, the youthful "figure of capable imagination" of "Mrs. Alfred Uruguay": models of the man who turns from the real to make of his imagination an interior kingdom: the vice-president of the Hartford Insurance Co., mutatis mutandis. The speaker of Ashbery's poem regards even such a figure as this, who maintains the shreds of his sublime identity through his self-subsisting interiority, from a dubious distance. The hero stands out against the eternality of nature, rapt in his own eternality, possessed by the futurity of his endless imagination. "But that has faded / Like flowers, like the first days // Of good conduct." The poet is no longer even behaving himself to Stevens's extent; instead such an identity can only be visited and pinched—in the sense of teasing, and in the sense of testing its reality. No wonder there appears no end to the hero's dislike! So early in his career Ashbery is already on tour, making excursions from one stance to another, without making distinctions or value judgments. But as he says before describing the visionary landscape of "Chaos" (and the title is painfully ironic, for the land exhibits a terrible sense of order): "Don't ask me to go there again." The one place to which Ashbery feels compelled to return is the one which unsettles him the most, the source of his greatest psychic threat and most bountiful linguistic powers.

This is the place of "These Lacustrine Cities" (from *Rivers and Mountains*), where Ashbery directly confronts the forces of human history for what is perhaps the only time in his entire career. Many of Ashbery's later successes come from his achievement in this poem; the metaphysical resolution and rhetorical closure he wrests from history here in turn provide the basis for the unique self-consciousness of subsequent volumes, the well-known "fence-sitting / Raised to the level of an esthetic ideal." For it seems to me that in this poem Ashbery is attempting to recapitulate the movement of history from the standpoint of art, telling the story of man's production of himself in relation to the role of the poet in society. In this regard, the poem is certainly an off-shoot of the sublime tradition, but in sublimely questioning the existential use of human effort, it arrests the process of its own making and relegates all subsequent utterance to merely aesthetic gestures.

The poem opens with two stanzas of remarkable force, which convince through their generalizing rhetoric:

> These lacustrine cities grew out of loathing
> Into something forgetful, although angry with history.
> They are the product of an idea: that man is horrible, for instance,
> Though this is only one example.
>
> They emerged until a tower
> Controlled the sky, and with artifice dipped back
> Into the past for swans and tapering branches,
> Burning, until all that hate was transformed into useless love.[38]

The city is the locus of civilization: art, science, commerce, industry all develop where geography has accommodated human labor.[39] But these cities are conscious only of loathing, for the work of civilization requires, on the individual level, the repression and re-channeling of desire; and on the social level, the alienation of labor from its potential for gratification and the creation of a class structure. In short, the cities wish to forget the necessity that brought them into existence but cannot, and hence are angry with history—and with themselves. Ashbery's ironic "Though this is only one example," as if he were a scholar or lecturer addressing a post-historical audience, makes the situation all the more bitter, since the notion of *progress* in the building of these cities is simply bypassed. Furthermore, the city-building seems to have ceased, and to borrow the central term of David Rigsbee's essay on the poem, the cities have instead created a monument to themselves in the form of the tower.[40] Historical processes have been arrested and we approach the present with dizzying speed, which is only natural in a place of forgetfulness.[41] The products of culture are transformed into commodities in a complete act of reification; all becomes artifice; and the nostalgic, fin-de-siècle image of "swans and tapering branches" signifies the decadent world of genteel consumption, the narcissistic satisfaction of "useless love."

No wonder then that the poet, the "you" of the poem, is left only "with an idea of yourself / And the feeling of ascending emptiness of the afternoon." Because he attempts to maintain the mentality of inwardness that is the sine qua non of the artist in bourgeois society, he is an embarrassment, marginalized, but perhaps still enough of a threat to require "all-inclusive plans" of the paternalistic "we" who addresses him. The poet's capitulation to this psychic despotism is a fait accompli:

> We had thought, for instance, of sending you to the middle of the
>   desert,
>
> To a violent sea, or having the closeness of the others be air
> To you, pressing you back into a startled dream
> As sea-breezes greet a child's face.
> But the past is already here, and you are nursing some private
>   project.

Whether through actual exile or the more insidious imposition of a condition of anomie, the poet becomes lost in the past that is always present, capable only of "nursing some private project"—yet another fit description of Ashbery's entire poetic enterprise. The Kafkaesque terror of "The worst is not over, yet I know / You will be happy here" is mitigated somehow, given Ashbery's subsequent development into a master of introspective self-absorption, but for all that, the poem's final admission of the loss of the sublime is genuinely chilling:

You have built a mountain of something
Thoughtfully pouring all your energy into this single monument,
Whose wind is desire starching a petal,
Whose disappointment broke into a rainbow of tears.

Just as the processes of history have been reified through the image of
the tower, so too the poetic processes are reified in "this single monu-
ment"—this poem, if not the entire oeuvre. The Shelleyan wind that
blows through such poetry has been stripped of its visionary power (it is
only "desire starching a petal"), but the poetry is so obsessed with its loss
that its disappointment in itself is beautiful, "a rainbow of tears." Ash-
bery gave another poem in *Rivers and Mountains* the title "Civilization and
Its Discontents," but the name could stand in for "These Lacustrine
Cities" as well.

The "private project" that Ashbery has nursed in all his books since
Rivers and Mountains is thus a vastly diminished version of the sublime.
His language maintains its historical resonance through its negations: he
hints at what his conception of poetry is by providing endless examples
of what it is not. As he says in "Grand Galop":

And one is left sitting in the yard
To try to write poetry
Using what Wyatt and Surrey left around,
Took up and put down again
Like so much gorgeous raw material
As though it would always happen in some way.[42]

This snickering self-consciousness reaches its absurd limits in *Houseboat
Days*, in such poems as "The Explanation," "And *Ut Pictura Poesis* is Her
Name" and "What is Poetry"; but it must be recognized as the necessary
complement to the more moving, even wrenching, moments of
awareness that reach their peak in "Self-Portrait in a Convex Mirror." In
Burke's terms, the poet's frequent turns to the ridiculous are intended to
deny the authority of the sublime; apparently the psychic risk involved
in appropriating the confrontational language of awe and power has
become too great. Nowhere is this more starkly demonstrated than in the
strange one-line poems in *As We Know*, in which the titles refer to one
term in the dialectic, the verses to the other:

The Cathedral Is   [sublime]

Slated for demolition.[43]   [ridiculous]

or

We Were On the Terrace
Drinking Gin and Tonics   [ridiculous]

when the squall hit.[44]   [sublime]

The ironic turns made by these miniatures are based entirely on the
tension and ambivalence we have noted throughout Ashbery's work. In
the first, we are led to expect lofty utterance, but that possibility is
literally demolished. In the second, bourgeois pleasures of the most
banal sort are interrupted by the threat of an outside power that Burke
sees as the source of the sublime.[45]

If in recent volumes there have been fewer approaches to the sublime,
it may be because Ashbery is wearying of the vacillation, and opting
instead for the recording of leveled mental processes that has always
been part of his stock-in-trade. Many critics see this tendency as precisely
that which makes Ashberry so important a poet for our time; I take
Altieri as their representative when he says of the work in general that

> There is no dream of a purified language. In fact, impurity of lan-
> guage becomes a mark of authenticity, since it registers the poet's
> awareness of the duplicity of discourse and the complexity of inten-
> tions. In impurity is our freedom and our salvation.[46]

It would seem that the existential equivalent to this deliberate impurity
of discourse is Ashbery's supposed lesson that "if the arbitrary limits of
one's life history are accepted absolutely, without regrets or even imag-
ined alternatives, the value and interest of that life history will come to
seem almost infinite."[47] But Ashbery himself, who can be monstrous in
his self-consciousness, appears to contradict this when, speaking of his
poems as "Marchenbilder," he declares:

> I want to go back, out of the bad stories,
> But there's always the possibility that the next one . . .
> No, it's another almond tree, or a ring-swallowing frog . . .
> Yet they are beautiful as we people them
>
> With ourselves. They are empty as cupboards.[48]

Nothing seems to have changed since his earliest exercises in am-
bivalence, except for the mastery of tone, which has probably meant
more to him in terms of his art than even the evasion of the sublime.
Even so, we continue to be in the midst of a "Worsening Situation":

> Like a rainstorm, he said, the braided colors
> Wash over me and are no help. Or like one

> At a feast who eats not, for he cannot choose
> From among the smoking dishes. This severed hand
> Stands for life, and wander as it will,
> East or west, north or south, it is ever
> A stranger who walks beside me. O seasons,
> Booths, chaleur, dark-hatted charlatans
> On the outskirts of some rural fete,
> The name you drop and never say is mine, mine!
> Some day I'll claim to you how all used up
> I am because of you but in the meantime the ride
> Continues. . . .[49]

Such a beautiful passage makes one appreciate the poignancy of Ashbery's ideological situation, of which this is a precise description. Unlike most contemporary poets, Ashbery remains graced with a sense of the infinite, but it is the "bad infinity" that the reification of bourgeois social relations imposes on those poets most conscious of the sublime and its demands. Ashbery is present at the feast but cannot eat; his hand is severed and can never reach out to the stranger who is, of course, himself; his is the name that is never said, though it is certainly dropped enough. Ashbery is almost never discussed in religious terms, but the desire for immanent meaning is so great in lines such as these that one is reminded of Marx's description of religion as "the soul of a soulless world." And if poetry such as Ashbery's has replaced religion for many intellectuals in our time, then perhaps we can find new meaning in this famous passage from "Self-Portrait in a Convex Mirror":

> The secret is too plain. The pity of it smarts,
> Makes hot tears spurt: that the soul is not a soul,
> Has no secret, is small, and it fits
> Its hollow perfectly: its room, our moment of attention.
> That is the tune but there are no words.
> The words are only speculation
> (From the Latin *speculum*, mirror):
> They seek and cannot find the meaning of the music.[50]

For Ashbery's world is finally not one so much of alienation as of soullessness.

Or is it? Marjorie Perloff, in observing the fact that Ashbery did not write an elegy for his friend Frank O'Hara, claims that it would be unlike Ashbery because "his is a poetic mode that absorbs personality into larger metaphysical structures."[51] But perhaps he has, despite himself. The poem is called "Street Musicians":

One died, and the soul was wrenched out
Of the other in life, who, walking the streets
Wrapped in an identity like a coat, sees on and on
The same corners, volumetrics, shadows
Under trees. . . .[52]

The New Arcady

The woods of Arcady are dead,
And over is their antique joy;
Of old the world on dreaming fed;
Grey Truth is now her painted toy;
But still she turns her restless head

—W. B. Yeats,
"The Song of the Happy Shepherd"

remembering powers of love
    and of poetry,
the Berkeley we believed
    grove of Arcady—

that there might be
    potencies in common things,
"princely manipulations of the real"

—Robert Duncan,
"A Poem Slow Beginning"

If the sublime comes to be regarded as an increasingly less viable mode of poetic discourse in New York in the Fifties and Sixties, then an attempt to revive it takes place at the same time across the country in Berkeley. Robert Duncan stands at the center of the so-called San Francisco Renaissance; and along with such firmly established figures as Charles Olson and Allen Ginsberg, he represents a deliberate return to the poet's vatic role, based on an unprecedented synthesis of Romantic and Modernist strategies. Duncan in particular has declared himself derivative in his craft, thus affording himself "permission" to create the frequently outrageous totalities that mark his poetry as one of the most ambitious bodies of work in our time. For Duncan's poetic is totalizing; to an even greater extent than Pound or Olson, he seeks to in-form the "orders" or "scales" of reality in an open-ended tapestry or collage of language. In this regard, he operates in exact antithesis to Ashbery and O'Hara: he seeks to establish, or rather, prove, that the interrelated

networks of material, psychological, and spiritual realities are all coordi-
nated hierarchies that function under the force of universal Law.[1]
Rather than level modes of perception, value systems and forms of
knowledge, Duncan would place them all within their proper contexts,
so that an awareness of overarching Form allows the reader to perceive a
previously hidden totality. Poetry, of course, is the most significant me-
dium for such a process; hence the poet holds a privileged place within
the orders of language. Duncan's thought is transparently utopian in
regard to matters of creativity and tradition, as well as in relation to
immediate political concerns; and while sometimes problematic in its
applications, its insistence on infinite human potential within a commu-
nal identity is, as Oppen would say, "ennobling." As Duncan declares in
"Orders," *Passages* 24:

> There is no
>
> good a man has in his own things except
>
> it be in the community of every thing;
>
> no nature he has
>
> but in his nature hidden in the heart of the living
>
> in the great household.[2]

Duncan's insistent metaphors are often so compelling that they seem
to obviate criticism, and therefore it is important to observe that at the
same time Duncan's totalizing project is getting under way, a related but
in some ways radically dissimilar poetic is being formulated by his old
friend—and critic—Jack Spicer. Cranky, admonitory, haunted, Spicer's
work presents as unified a poetic as Duncan's, but carefully avoids the
sweeping gestures of order and coherence that have become the dis-
tinguishing mark of even the most open of Duncan's poetic fields.
Spicer's sincere distrust of the totalizing impulse in both Romantic and
Modernist poetry leads him to a poetic of disruption and difference, of
radical otherness and possession, in which the poet is far less the willing
spokesman for the sublime than its unsuspecting victim. Whereas Dun-
can celebrates the "Lasting Sentence" in his *Structure of Rime,* Spicer
warns us, in *The Heads of the Town Up to the Aether,* that "words / Turn
mysteriously against those who use them." In fact, it could be argued
that Duncan and Spicer draw upon the same poetic precursors and
philosophical systems and create complementary views of the poetic act.
For Duncan, Romantic myth-making and theosophical doctrine combine
with Modernist explorations of history, anthropology and phe-
nomenology to confirm Yeats's old dictum that "The things below are as
the things above." For Spicer the Romantics' demonic subjectivity, the

dualities of the gnostics and the Modernists' fragmentation of lyric and
narrative all yield the equally Yeatsian notion that "there is a deep enmity
between a man and his destiny."[3]

Both poets then are certainly dedicated to reviving a vision of the
sublime; and both share, however doubtfully, in poetry's utopian pro-
pensity. Like Ashbery in "These Lacustrine Cities," Spicer offers a highly
condensed and elliptical retelling of the dialectic of civilization and
poetry in the "Textbook of Poetry" section of *The Heads of the Town:*

> the city that we create in our bartalk or in our fuss
> and fury about each other is in an utterly mixed and
> mirrored way an image of the city. A return from exile.[4]

Spicer has Dante's exile from Florence in mind, but must also be con-
scious of the "Heavenly City, Earthly City" envisioned by Duncan more
than ten years before:

> In the moment of song—earthly radiant
> city of poetry—that golden light
> consumes in its focus a world I have sufferd,
> the darkend city of my perishable age.[5]

And although Spicer doubts, as Duncan himself comes to doubt, that the
utopian city or the new Arcady could be built among the Bohemian
poets of San Francisco, both poets maintain that we must, as Spicer says,

> Hold to the future. With firm hands. The future of
> each afterlife, of each ghost, of each word that is
> about to be mentioned.[6]

Because both poets pay great attention to "each word that is about to
be mentioned," it can be said that the very notion of futurity in their
work is closely related to the models of poetic inspiration to which they
constantly refer. Spicer and Duncan are two of the leading practitioners
among contemporary poets of poetry as poetics, which is to say that they
attain that high level of self-consciousness necessary to relate their work
as individuals to the ongoing activity of poetry as a historical continuum.
One such moment of recognition occurs in the first letter to Lorca in
Jack Spicer's *After Lorca* (1957), that disquieting book in which Spicer
attempts to remake himself into the poet he wishes to be. He does so by
giving himself up to the *daimon* (as Yeats would call him) or *duende* (as
Lorca himself would call him), and thus speaks with an authority he
previously lacked. He assumes a traditional stance, and with wonderful
irony speaks of tradition itself:

In my last letter [though this is the first letter Spicer writes] I spoke of
the tradition. The fools that read these letters will think by this we
mean what tradition seems to have meant lately—an historical patch-
work (whether made up of Elizabethan quotations, guide books of the
poet's home town, or obscure hints of obscure bits of magic published
by Pantheon) which is used to cover up the nakedness of the bare
word. Tradition means much more than that. It means generations of
different poets in different countries patiently telling the same story,
writing the same poem, gaining and losing something with each trans-
formation—but, of course, never really losing anything. This has
nothing to do with calmness, classicism, temperament, or anything
else. Invention is merely the enemy of poetry.[7]

Spicer's vision of generations of poets is one of the most recent formula-
tions of a venerable idea. Among poets writing in English, its spokesmen
have included such major (and diverse) figures as Shelley, Yeats, Pound
and Eliot, all of whom would agree that poets are always "writing the
same poem," with invention always "the enemy of poetry."[8]
    Much the same is true for Duncan in *The Truth & Life of Myth:*

Myth, for Dante, for Shakespeare, for Milton, was the poet-lore
handed down in the tradition from poet to poet. It was the very matter
of Poetry, the nature of the divine world as poets had testified to it; the
poetic piety of each poet, his acknowledgement of what he had found
true Poetry, worked to conserve that matter. And, for each, there was
in the form of their work—the literary vision, the play of actors upon
the stage, and the didactic epic—a kind of magic, for back of these
forms we surmise distant origins in the rituals toward ecstasy of
earliest Man.[9]

Tradition here is a source of primal empowerment: it can provide the
individual poet with a transpersonal, communal authority that will allow
him to articulate his own contribution to the ongoing matter of the
historical work. Duncan's open fields (*Passages, The Structure of Rime,* etc.)
and Spicer's "books" can both be seen as attempts to find contemporary
correlatives to the historically appropriate forms of a Dante, a Shake-
speare, a Milton. They seek to respond to the demands of the moment,
knowing full well that in doing so, they intuitively respond to the move-
ment of history as one moment opens on to the next:

One of the disciplines I have struggled to achieve and struggle still to
achieve is a quickness to recognize shifts in the nature of the work, to
stop, even in mid-air, when I have lost the feel, for the reality of the
poem—the creative nexus or the true poem that moves the poem—is
the source, not the product, of my working there.[10]

Spicer, who tends to avoid such grand pronouncements, still says much
the same thing in recounting the experience of the "dictated" poem:

> suddenly there comes a poem which you just hate and would like to
> get rid of that says just exactly opposite of what you mean, of what you
> have to say. You want to say something about your beloved's eyebrows
> and the poem says the eyes should fall out. And you don't really want
> the eyes to fall out. Or, you're trying to write a poem about Viet Nam
> and you write a poem about Vermont. These things, again, begin to
> show you just exactly where the road to dictation leads.[11]

Although both poets wish to open their poems to the incoming future
(what Bloch calls "the *still underived derivation* of all that happens"[12]),
there remains the crucial difference between them that we have already
cited: the difference between the mage and the medium, the domestic
householder and the barroom heckler, the Logos and the Lowghost. In a
revealing passage from *The Truth & Life of Myth,* Duncan explains one of
his models for inspiration and composition:

> Speaking of a thing I call upon its name, and the Name takes over
> from me the story I would tell, if I let the dimmest realization of that
> power enter here. But the myth we are telling is the myth of the power
> of the Word. The Word, as we refer to It, undoes all the bounds of
> semantics we would draw in Its creative need to realize Its true Self. It
> takes over. Its desire would take over and seem to put out or to drown
> the individual reality—lonely invisible and consumed flame in the
> roaring light of the Sun—but Its creativity moves in all the realities
> and can only realize Itself in the Flesh, in the incarnation of concrete
> and mortal Form.[13]

Significantly, Duncan *lets* the power enter and begin its work; mutuality
and reciprocity are established between the individual and the Word.
"Things," i.e., material reality, move the poet; such inspiration estab-
lishes the connection between consciousness and the otherwise distant
sublime. The sense of continuity that Duncan is able to establish in his
poetry, the totality of effort that encompasses even the most diverse
content, may be traced back to his personal sense of confidence as
expressed in this idea of inspiration. For Duncan, the world will respond
to the responsive poet ("the Poet on Guard," as he calls him in an early
poem); and even in the midst of the most severe personal or political
crisis, apprehensions of universal order inevitably appear:

> I thought to come into an open room
> where in the south light of afternoon
> one I was improvised
> passages of changing dark and light

> a music dream and passion would have playd
> to illustrate concords of order in order,
> a contrapuntal communion of all things[14]

How different this is from Spicer's view of inspiration! Although Spicer does speak of allowing the "outside" to come through, and even suggests that there may be means for a poet to facilitate such a process, in the end there is little that is benign or ordered in the way the poem comes to the poet. On the contrary, because Spicer's model is derived from gnostic sources, in which the sublime truth always resides beyond the limits of human knowledge and belief, the poem is inevitably the result of hostility, "An argument between the dead and the living," in which "The poet thinks continually of strategies, of how he can win out against the poem."[15] Spicer frequently conflates his idea of sublime, dictated utterance with "the dead," that is, history and the poetic tradition, which are always beyond the understanding of the individual poet—despite the fact that the messages somehow get through. This is a view that coalesces in such early works as *After Lorca* and the *Imaginary Elegies*, finds its fullest articulation in *The Heads of the Town*, and is painfully confirmed in the last books, such as *Language* and the *Book of Magazine Verse*. Consider "Sporting Life," from *Language:*

> The trouble with comparing a poet with a radio is that radios don't develop scar-tissue. The tubes burn out, or with a transistor, which most souls are, the battery or diagram burns out replaceable or not replaceable, but not like that punchdrunk fighter in the bar. The poet
> Takes too many messages. The right to the ear that floored him in New Jersey. The right to say that he stood six rounds with a champion.
> Then they sell beer or go on sporting commissions, or, if the scar tissue is too heavy, demonstrate in a bar where the invisible champions might not have hit him. Too many of them.
> The poet is a radio. The poet is a liar. The poet is a counterpunching radio.
> And those messages (God would not damn them) do not even know they are champions.[16]

Spicer's figure of the poet as "counterpunching radio" indicates the extent to which he goes to demonstrate the wanton power of poetic dictation, the arbitrary choosing of the poet (as opposed to permission or election) and the utterly alien quality of the poems themselves.[17] These "messages," as Spicer calls them, are meant to be regarded as impersonal linguistic structures, despite the very personal effect they may have on poet or reader. Meaning dissolves in a typical Spicer poem because the source of meaning becomes increasingly distanced; thus nonsense and confession, satire and lyricism are always so oddly juxtaposed. The poet is alternately gleeful and appalled, for as in the best "nonsense" poems of Lewis Carroll or Edward Lear, the ghost of meaning is alternately playful or out for revenge. Spicer sees no alternative to such a situation, and in contrast to Duncan, his utopian propensity takes as its premise its simultaneous emergence and loss:

> We shall build our city backwards from each baseline extending
>   like a square ray from each distance—you from the first-base
>   line, you from behind the second baseman, you from behind the
>   short stop, you from the third-baseline.
> We shall clear the trees back, the lumber of our pasts and futures
>   back, because we are on a diamond, because it is our diamond
> Pushed forward from.
> And our city shall stand as the lumber rots and Runcible mountain
>   crumbles, and the ocean, eating all of islands, comes to meet
>   us.[18]

What for Duncan endures and grows, perpetuating itself in all creative acts, for Spicer becomes a momentary gesture, heroic only in its resignation, as it shimmers and disappears.

Perhaps the most efficient means to demonstrate these similarities and differences is to choose two exemplary texts, one by Duncan, one by Spicer, and consider the ways in which their varied acts of inspired composition seek to fulfill utopian desire. But such an orderly method must be qualified immediately, given the consistent structuring of both poets' mature work. Duncan's poems become increasingly more difficult to delimit as time goes on: not only do the ongoing *Passages* and *Structure of Rime* blur the textual borders between discrete volumes, but key themes and linguistic motifs appear with greater regularity in an ever expanding series of personal, literary and philosophical contexts. Furthermore, because of his stance as a derivative poet, Duncan deliberately blurs his own poetic ideas into those of his precursors and contemporaries, until a communal voice is heard, intoning a unified body of poetic revelation.[19] One chooses a Duncan poem for an old-fashioned "close reading"—even when in search of new themes—at the risk of violating the very premises upon which *all* of the poetry is based.

The same is true of any of Spicer's books, though for different reasons. Because Spicer views the poet as an arbitrarily chosen medium, for whom the serial poem is a sequence of momentarily illuminated rooms in an otherwise darkened house,[20] there is no guaranteed sense of organic coherence to be discovered by the assiduous close reader of an individual Spicer book, despite the fact that Spicer indicated the book or serial poem to be the generic measure of his work. On the contrary, Spicer's theories of inspiration and poetic structure are designed to allow for and even invite frequent disruptions, the entrance of mediumistic voices that completely undermine any stated purpose or theme in the text. As Peter Riley points out, Spicer's books can be regarded as a progression from a concern with "a singular obsessive figure (Billy the Kid, Rimbaud, etc.)," through "a *field* of reference (Arthurian romance)," to "his final ability to operate a book beyond obsession or preoccupation altogether . . . the complete book without any external defining or colouring factors, which he first did with *Language*."[21] This means that Spicer's rapid maturation, like that far more gradual process in Duncan's career, is pointed in the direction of poetic totality, in which even the seemingly most random elements dispersed in the field call to and beyond each other, until the text completely deconstructs its prescribed boundaries.

Hence the insistence on the part of both poets that the work is ultimately a collage, an infinite set of correspondences. Here is Duncan's articulation of the concept, from the Introduction to *Bending the Bow:*

> *It* is striving to come into existence in these things, or, all striving to come into existence is It—in this realm of men's languages a poetry of all poetries, *grand collage,* I name It, having only the immediate events of words to speak for It.[22]

And here is Spicer's, in one of the letters to Lorca:

> The poem is a collage of the real. . . .
> Things do not connect; they correspond. That is what makes it possible for a poet to translate real objects, to bring them across language as easily as he can bring them across time. That tree you saw in Spain is a tree I could never have seen in California, that lemon has a different smell and a different taste, BUT the answer is this—every place and every time has a real object to *correspond* with your real object—that lemon may become this lemon, or it may even become this piece of seaweed, or this particular color of gray in this ocean. One does not need to imagine that lemon; one needs to discover it.[23]

When Duncan argues for a poetry of all poetries and Spicer claims that a lemon may correspond to a piece of seaweed or the gray of the ocean, they apparently foreclose on any New Critical interpretations of their work. As Gerald Graff says of New Criticism,

> Taking account of objective reality is identified with passive adjustment to the status quo, with the mass man's drugged acceptance of his

status as a manipulable object. For the New Critics, it follows that
literature must be defined as a self-sufficient world, not a mere repre-
sentation of an already existing one.[24]

In contrast, the art of collage as practiced by Duncan and Spicer is most
purely the art of the possible. Rather than consolidate temporal and
spatial relations into self-sufficient worlds, they insist that the very notion
of self-sufficiency is impossible, given the means by which their poetry
comes into existence. No single meaning, however complex or ambigu-
ous, can be sufficient; the text's polysemous nature not only summons
other meanings, but other texts as well. As Duncan declares:

> and only in the imagination of the Whole
>   the immediate percept is
>   to be justified— Imagining
>   this
>   pivot of a totality
>   having
>   no total thing in us, we so
>   live beyond ourselves
>
>   —and in this   unitive.[25]

But if we reverse Duncan's declaration, it remains to be seen whether
"the immediate percept" justifies "the imagination of the Whole." Again
and again in the reading of both poets, certain more or less discrete
poems and fragments impose themselves upon the imagination: the
work is not of a piece in its actual execution, and textual boundaries insist
upon being drawn. *Language,* for example, is simply not as strong as *The
Heads of the Town* or *The Holy Grail;* despite the evocative force of
individual poems, the play of correspondences seems too diffuse; and
one is forced to concede that Spicer needed the concentration of his
"obsessions" in order to take dictation most successfully. And in all of
Duncan's volumes, including the recent *Ground Work,* certain individual
poems, no matter how complex within themselves or related to accom-
panying pieces, provide the greatest satisfaction. When Duncan's work is
anthologized, it is "Often I Am Permitted To Return To A Meadow,"
"This Place Rumord To Have Been Sodom" or "A Poem Beginning With
A Line By Pindar" (from *The Opening of the Field*) or "My Mother Would
Be A Falconress" (from *Bending the Bow*) that editors select; and it is
worth considering that Spicer's work has not been adequately repre-
sented in anthologies because editors have yet to learn that one of his
single, cohesive books is the best demonstration of his genius. Is it only in
principle, then, that the work as grand collage can be defended?

Unfortunately, there is no simple response to such a question. If it is naive, given the nature of Duncan's or Spicer's enterprise, to simply "analyze" an individual poem, it is likewise naive to simply accept the paralyzing binary opposition between scrupulous New Critical interpretation of "well wrought urns" and dizzying Postmodern proclamations of intertextuality and open form. The open / closed dichotomy which so bedevils the critics in their discourses on such poetry seems to bother the poets to a much smaller extent. If one is really composing in accordance with the "content under hand" (the phrase is Charles Olson's), then the poem must follow the contours of thought and feeling: form of any sort cannot be prescribed, but will reveal itself to the reader as both necessary and appropriate. This is what Duncan means when he speaks of the "Form of Forms," "the wholeness of a poem in which all of its parts are redeemed as meaning."[26]

Consider Duncan's recent "Circulation of the Song." This magnificent poem, which appears at the end of *Ground Work,* is notable for its unusually self-sustained form, consistency of tone and voice, and completed (rather than fragmentary) syntax. It is built upon a clearly delineated stanza structure and makes use of a relatively limited and accessible set of literary allusions and references. It is a particularly striking contrast to the other major efforts in *Ground Work,* such as "Poems from the Margins of Thom Gunn's *Moly,*" "A Seventeenth Century Suite" and "Dante Etudes," all of which are derivations and re-workings of freely acknowledged precursor texts; or the *Tribunals* sections of *Passages,* which, like earlier sections of that poem, make extensive use of quotation, allusion and spatialized fields of reference. The subtitle of "Circulations of the Song" is simply "After Jalai Al-Din Rumi," though Rumi's presence in the poem is totally subsumed by Duncan's own persistent, and by now easily identified tone. What's more, the poem is much less overtly self-reflexive than most of Duncan's mature work: although it does speak to questions of its own inspiration and composition, it is equally concerned with the connections between the poet's religious beliefs, his long-standing relationship to his lover, and his sense of himself as he grows old. Like the deeply moving "My Mother Would Be A Falconress," its rich lyric diction may be correlated to a largely interior, subjective project which Duncan often calls "essential autobiography." In short, it is, at least on the surface, a far more conventional, "bounded" poem than Duncan is wont to write.

Yet "Circulations of the Song" confirms every important idea that Duncan has developed in regard to his poetic practice, and renews the utopian sense of openness and possibility that makes his best work so important:

I am like a line cast out
    into a melodic unfolding beyond itself
      a mind hovering ecstatic
above a mouth in which the heart rises
    pouring itself into liquid and fiery speech
for the sake of a rime not yet arrived
    containing again and again resonant arrivals.[27]

Here the poet is both a subjective force of ecstatic inspiration and an objective vehicle for that inspiration, whose words are perpetual preparations for "a rime not yet arrived," a poetry of pure futurity. But this ecstatic awareness is tempered by Duncan's increasing certainty of his own mortality. Thus the *He* of the poem, the dark homosexual Eros who consecrates the poet's marriage to his lover, is also a god of death; and the fulfillment of the sexual relationship is a premonition of that final fulfillment:

                How has your face
aged over these years to keep company with mine?
ever anew as I waken endearing.   Each night
    in the exchange of touch and speech blessing,

prepared thruout for rest.   Is it not
as if He were almost here?   as if we were

        already at rest?[28]

Physical beauty and the confidence of youth likewise pass into such knowledge:

    For a moment did Beauty pass over my face?
    I did not have to reach for *your* beauty.
    Radiant, it entirely flowd out and thru me.[29]

Because of this, Duncan's relationship to his muse is all the more fierce and perilous:

    Again you have instructed me to let go,
    to hold to this falling,   this
        letting myself go.
    I will succumb entirely to your intention.

        Contend with me!
    you demand. And I am surrounded by wingd
        confusions. *He*
    is everywhere,   nowhere
        now where I am.

> In every irreality there is Promise.
> But there
> where I am not　　*He*　　really is.
>
> 　In Whose Presence
> it is as if I had a new name.[30]

This passage is yet another restatement of one of Duncan's central myths, Jacob's wrestling with the angel, which permeates both his poetry *(The Opening of the Field)* and criticism *(The Truth & Life of Myth)*. This poetic fiction, or "irreality," is especially full of hope. The erotic physical contact with the divinely beautiful and the linguistic revelation that follows in Jacob's being renamed Israel have always attracted Duncan, but now the stakes are higher: as he ages he must give himself over more completely to struggle, confusion, and the intention of the Absolute. For Duncan such contention has always been equated with composition, and the shaping of the present poem comes to vindicate his faith. Yet this does not entail a merely personal expression of religious belief, or even the confirmation of the poet's metaphysical grounding of aesthetic doctrine. As Duncan concludes:

> 　　　　In the Grand Assemblage of Lives,
> 　　　the Great Assembly-House,
> this Identity, this Ever-Presence,　　arranged
> 　　rank for rank,　　person for person,　　each from its own
> sent out from what we were　　to another place
> 　　now in the constant exchange
>
> 　　renderd true.[31]

What begins as personal revelation is made into a concrete universal, not to be asserted in abstraction, but to be re-enacted in lived experience—including the encounter with linguistic form.

In composing a poem such as "Circulations of the Song," a poem capable of demonstrating that "all of its parts are redeemed as meaning," Duncan implicitly transcends the open / closed dichtomoy that can be found close to the heart of any discussion of his work. The totality that he would teach us to see, "the Grand Assemblage of Lives," emerges in an orderly and indeed, self-sufficient manner, without sacrificing, but rather heeding, the demands of perpetually unfolding events. In his own way, Spicer comes to this point too, the correspondences he is driven to seek ordering themselves under the psychic pressures of what Robin Blaser calls "the practice of outside." *The Holy Grail* is worth considering in this regard, for it is, again, a less self-reflexive work than *The Heads of the Town,* while still achieving a marvelous balance between

internal ordering and external "Orders." Peter Riley's essay on the book
amply demonstrates its internal consistence; his structuralist analysis,
based on the text's seven-fold arrangements of form and theme, while
not always consistent with my reading of individual characters and
poems, shows how hermetic, autonomous and even organically consist-
ent a poem can be written following Spicer's theories of composition. But
the narrative boundaries that *The Holy Grail* establishes for itself, its
numerological scaffolding, its skeleton of Arthurian reference, are also
designed to permit their violation, their periodic invasions by voices that
vindicate the structure by denying the coherence of its purposiveness.
Reading *The Holy Grail* provides an awareness of poetry's dialectical
identity as structure and process, an awareness that serves as a necessary
corrective to most modern critical paradigms.

This is nowhere more apparent than in Spicer's contrast of poetry and
the grail near the beginning of the book. According to Spicer's revision
of the tale,

> The grail is the opposite of poetry
> Fills us up instead of using us as a cup the dead drink from.
> The grail the cup Christ bled into and the cup of plenty in Irish
>   mythology
> The poem. Opposite. Us. Unfulfilled.
> These worlds make the friendliness of human to human seem
>   close as cup to lip.
> Savage in their pride the beasts pound around the forest
>   perilous.[32]

Poetry and the grail are seen as opposites because poetry fills us with the
living voices of the dead, while the religious experience of the Absolute,
as symbolized by the grail, drains us of our individual subjectivity, as we
are consumed by the rituals of what is dead and past. But in either event
we are merely vessels, and as such, unfulfilled. This careful equation is
abruptly thrown off balance by the last two sentences of the poem,
which, in a sense, come in from outside to comment on the previous
statements. (In *The Heads of the Town*, Spicer uses the device of the
"Explanatory Notes" to comment on the statements in the "Homage to
Creeley" section. In *The Holy Grail*, statement and commentary, haunted
and haunter, are condensed into a single text.) The "worlds" refer to
poetry and religion, both of which detach us from ordinary human
contact—friendship, including the heroic camaraderie of the grail
knights, becomes as casual and fleeting as cup held to lip. Ironically, *we*
are the cup, again merely a vessel, and hence the original statement of
the poem is reinforced by the ghostly intrusion. The last sentence con-
firms the message even more dramatically. For an apparent non se-

quitur, it is voiced with sublime confidence, like all the non sequiturs in *The Holy Grail*. The intrusive voice itself is savage in its pride, like the beasts which will threaten the grail knights as they enter the forest perilous. In other words, this last sentence, in its disconnectedness and nonchalance, reminds us of our fate as knightly or poetic questers. Poetry or the Absolute will undo us, expose the egotism of our quests, and make use of us for their own inscrutable purposes.

Spicer's antipathy to traditional shows of heroism as manifestations of the egotistical sublime, whether in knights or poets, may be found throughout his work. Duncan, with his love of grand gestures, is a frequent target, as in the early poem "For Robert" in *Admonitions* ("The poet / Robert D. / Writes poetry while we / Listen to him."), or the more vituperative piece in *Language* that begins "If you don't believe in a god, don't quote him." "Heroes eat soup like anyone else," declares Spicer, also in *Language,* but it is in *The Holy Grail* that heroes are humbled more than anywhere else in his opus. Even Galahad, purest of the knights, eventually discovers that "The Grail is as common as rats or seaweed," indicating that the network of correspondences that unmakes the order of the poem likewise unmakes any hierarchical order of belief. The other knights fare even more poorly, especially the hypocritical Lancelot, of whom it is said that "He has all the sense of fun of an orange," a blistering indictment given Spicer's love of jokes and wisecracks. His lover, Gwenivere, is granted some of the most poignant lines in the book, for unlike the knights, her only goal is love, which of course will finally be denied her. "The Book of Gwenivere" is the only section of *The Holy Grail* spoken entirely in the first person and addressed to a single, specific listener, Lancelot: there are no intrusive voices commenting on the stupidity of knightly deeds, but rather Gwenivere's own comments on the entire process:

> . . . Damn
> The ghosts of the unbent flame, the pixies, the kobalds, the
>   dwarves eating jewels underground, the lives that seem to have
>   nothing to do except to make you have
> Adventures.
> Naked I lie in this bed. The spooks
> Around me animate themselves.
> Boo! Hello!
> Lance, the cup is heavy. Drop the cup![33]

A woman forced to deal with male codes of chivalry and political intrigue, Gwenivere must also contend with the supernatural, which seems intent on disrupting whatever little solace she can attain, given her perilous situation. Her frank sexuality is a contrast to the presumably guilty, haunted Lancelot, but she cannot persuade him to drop the cup, that is, abandon the quest, for as she says, "Christ and this little teacup / Were always between us." Neither Lancelot's heroism nor courtesy impresses her; her disappointment pervades her every word and results in the most coherent section of the book.

The wisest and most painful section of *The Holy Grail*, however, belongs to Arthur, "Rex quondam et futurus with a banjo on my knee." Speaking from Avalon, which has "Supermarkets—where the dead trade bones with the dead," Arthur has been translated from the mortal sphere and sounds like a ghost himself. From his supernatural vantage point, Arthur is able to speak transhistorically; and he continually turns his regretful words against himself, disrupting any noble sentiments he might be tempted to utter:

> A noise in the head of the prince. A noise that travels a long ways
> Past chances, broken pieces of lumber,
> "Time future," the golden head said,
> "Time present. Time past."
> And the slumbering apprentice never dared tell the master. A
>   noise.
> It annoys me to look at this country. Dead branches. Leaves unable
>   even to grimly seize their rightful place in the tree of the heart
> Annoys me
> Arthur, king and future king
> A noise in the head of the prince. Something in God-language.
>   In spite of all this horseshit, this uncomfortable music.[34]

Once a king himself, unable to comprehend the "uncomfortable music" he heard, Arthur has now become only "A noise in the head of the prince," who, as the pun indicates, can only annoy some other ruler who will repeat the same stupid mistakes. This accounts for the reference to Robert Greene's play, as cited by Robin Blaser in "The Practice of Outside."[35] The brazen head speaks of eternity instead of history, but the alchemist has fallen asleep and cannot hear the message. One gets the message, as Arthur does, only when it is too late to be of help. Again, the voice that intrudes upon the poem guarantees its destruction and certifies its authenticity simultaneously, before it passes into the void.

The disquieting effect of the San Francisco poets' fascination with the supernatural, with arcane symbolism and mystical beliefs, is quite well known. Olson's famous criticism of San Francisco as "an école des Sages ou Mages"[36] reminds one now of Auden's description of Yeats as "the deplorable spectacle of a grown man occupied with the mumbo-jumbo of magic."[37] Olson, of course, was really as sympathetic to Duncan as

Auden was to Yeats, and Duncan later accepted a good deal of Olson's criticism.[38] But the distrust revealed by such remarks cannot be laid to rest, even when friendships are patched up or value grudgingly recognized. In a rational age, the critical faculty comes alive when it scents poetic "mumbo-jumbo," and the end result is generally disastrous for the offending poet—the present vogue for James Merrill notwithstanding. Even today, Yeats's supernatural beliefs are regarded with suspicion, despite numerous demonstrations of their essential role in the formation of the poems; and one cannot help but wonder if Duncan, despite his relative fame, remains something of a poet's poet because of his continued faith in the truth and life of myth. Twenty years after his death, Spicer remains the almost exclusive property of a small band of mainly West Coast poets and critics (most of whom misread him as a post-structuralist); and his work is poorly represented in Donald Allen's 1982 revision of *The New American Poetry, The Postmoderns*.[39] Elsewhere I have argued that Spicer's ghosts are metaphors for the poet's act of composition in relation to the tradition and to history itself; but I can offer no such argument for the beliefs of Spicer's and Duncan's old friend, Helen Adam. Adam, who was significantly eliminated from the revised Allen anthology, maintains her faith in reincarnation, karma and the animal-headed Egyptian deities Anubis and Bast, stating flatly that the muse is interested in little else:

> The loud cock-a-lo-runs, the rhymsters in fashion,
> The pallid professors who scribble of passion,
> The Media's mouth, the political poet,
> She cannot abide them, and one day they'll know it.
>
> Oh! stern, incorruptible, star gazing Muse,
> Be praised, and be blessed for the poets you choose.
> The poor, and the lonely, the strange are your choice.
> To the lost, and the mad, comes the heaven-sent voice.[40]

As Yeats pointed out, it was mostly London shop-girls who spent their shillings on the mediums he visited, and millions of working-class housewives continue to devour horoscopes today. The desire for knowledge and control in those denied access to legitimate institutions must express itself as it can. In much the same manner, the ballad form continues to survive despite its commercialization; and while Adam's work seems a throwback to a much earlier form of popular art, it is in fact a contemporary expression of certain emotional states that often find their clearest voice in the "rough" meters and violent imagery that characterize these poems.[41] (Duncan and Spicer have also had recourse to this form, no doubt under Adam's influence.) Moreover, Adam's elaborately over-determined relation to Romanticism indicates that she draws as much from high culture as low, leading us to conclude that such "mumbo-jumbo," when seen as a historically mediated phenomenon, signifies a great deal more than cloudy superstition. Magic, unlike religion, tends to resist institutionalization; it remains the resource of the marginalized ("The poor, and the lonely, the strange are your choice"). In this regard, magic and poetry have always been allied; and it makes perfect sense that when poetry becomes thoroughly domesticated, one of the most remarkable advocates of its passionate heritage should be a chanting, amulet-wearing prophetess, transplanted, in the company of her supportive sister, from the strictly patriarchal confines of her Scottish Presbyterian home to the exoticism of San Francisco.[42] Mingling with the flamboyant Duncan (whose work, it should be recalled, was thrown out of the *Kenyon Review* by John Crowe Ransom upon publication of "The Homosexual and Society") and the bar-cruising Spicer (who played the longshoreman to Duncan's aesthete), Adam knows precisely what she means when she ranks the poet and the outcast together. It is surely an old romantic pose, but its effect would no doubt be telling on thousands of young careerists in creative writing programs—if they were only exposed to it.

What is of moment here is the notion of possession and the passionate intensity it represents. The ghosts who broadcast messages through Spicer, turning him into a "counter-punching radio," gradually come to possess him—so much so that he can neither be self-possessed nor the possession of the culture industry and the stifling social relations that pertain to it. To be a poet, then, is to be possessed by passions that will brook no compromises, to be haunted by a desire which, when thwarted by historical circumstance, becomes all the more demonic when approached by normative social institutions. The value which utopian thinking places upon autonomy, on existential freedom, ironically turns into domination by psychic powers from "outside" self and society, leading to the destruction of both. Tragically, Spicer's biography as well as his poetry may be read according to this paradigm. Adam, whose personal identity and "aesthetic ideology" is more secure, completely narratizes the situation, projecting it into the fantastic realm in which all her social and psychological conflicts are secured: reified into "old-fashioned" ballads.

Thus, in "The House O'The Mirror," the woman who speaks the poem has a lover whose appetite is such that he would have her body and soul, desiring not only solace and sexual gratification, but the totality of her being. Both lovers are haunted by the reflection of the woman in the mirror: for the man, she is the unobtainable other he is compelled to dominate; for the woman, she is the ghost of her self, who maintains her assailed psychic integrity:

> But wae's my hert for well I ken
> He seeks a love ne'er found by men.
> Foredoomed, and damned, he seeks the lass
> Wha haunts the darkness o' the glass.
>
> The ghaist that in the mirror gleams,
> Floating aloof, like one wha dreams;
> For her he rages, mad and blind,
> And plunders a' my flesh to find.[43]

The frenzied sexuality of the lovers only heightens their awareness of the dilemma; the woman in particular realizes the inviolable nature of her supernatural reflection:

> Aye! though we strauchle breast to breast,
> And kiss sae hard we cry for rest,
> And daur a' pleasures till they cloy,
> We find nae peace, and little joy.
>
> For still between us stirs the shade
> That ne'er will lie beneath his plaid.
> A' but my ghaist tae him I give.
> My ghaist nae man may touch and live.

Although she partakes in earthly passion, capitulating to her own and her lover's bodily demands, she is simultaneously horrified by such entrapment, concluding that normative relations between man and woman would take from her the one thing she cannot give:

> My flesh is starvit morn and night
> For a' love's horror and delight.
> My ghaist apart frae passion stands;
> It is my ghaist that love demands.

The poem is open-ended in that the dilemma remains unresolved: the lovers will always be haunted, for the man will persist in his vain struggle, and the woman, caught in the relationship, will remain possessed by her reflection, the autonomous image of herself with which she can never be united. In some ways, the poem is an insidious revision of Yeats's "The Song of Wandering Aengus," a demystification by the pursued, enchanted woman of Aengus's idealistic quest. Likewise, it opens itself to a feminist reading, for love obviously means entrapment, domestication and existential loss; and the desire for autonomy leads to "hysteria." Also, the woman as well as the man perpetuates their irreconcilable conflict, for though he appears to her as a burning, rapacious demon who "shines and thunders on the hill" (as opposed to the reflection, "Floating aloof, like one wha dreams"), she returns his love with the same degree of ardor, due to what Dorothy Dinnerstein has accurately called "our sickened zest for the life of the flesh."[44] Commenting on the roles woman plays in normative heterosexual relations, Dinnerstein observes that

> She will be seen as naturally fit to nurture other people's individuality; as the born audience in whose awareness other people's subjective existence can be mirrored; as the being so peculiarly needed to confirm other people's worth, power, significance that if she fails to render them this service she is a monster, anomalous and useless. And at the same time she will also be seen as the one who will not let other people be, the one who beckons her loved ones back from selfhood, who wants to engulf, dissolve, drown, suffocate them as autonomous persons.[45]

Appropriately enough for Adam's persistently mirrored vision, the man is seen as the monster in the ballad, dissolving and drowning the woman's selfhood, though the woman is still expected to reflect his subjective existence, which she herself is denied.[46]

In another ballad, however, the woman literally hunts the man, who, already possessed by the muse, cannot yield to her demands. This is "The Birkenshaw," in which the Elf Queen, a figure of rapacious female sexuality, is denied the charms of the harper Robin o' Leith. A shape changer, Robin attempts to elude the Queen and her hunters, but, as is usually the case in such ballads, is run to ground. A final encounter ensues:

> "Bid fareweel tae your harp, Robin,
> Snap its strings wi' your hand.
> For I will keep ye a thousand years
> In my silent fairy land."

> "The strings o' my harp are strong, Lady.
> The strings o' my harp are strong.
> My harp has ridden a doomsday wave
> Wi' a mane a rainbow long.

> When I have broken its strings, Lady,
> The floods o' my hert will flow,
> As once they flowed for the truth o' love
> When I harped Atlantis low."[47]

What the Elf Queen fails to realize is that Robin's magic is greater than hers, for while her authority rests upon carnal desire, his is derived from the total possession of his art, which transcends any single ego. This power, which endures throughout history, ultimately consumes its bearer; hence the final transformation:

> She's seized on him wi' her arms sae cauld
> But he melted frae her clutch.
> He's changed his shape tae the holy harp,
> And that she daur na' touch.
>
> His sangs flew up like birds about her
> And blinded her wi' their wings,
> Till his banes became the base o' the harp
> And his hert became its strings.
>
> The harp stands in her hollow mountain,
> And whiles the harp will sing.
> Pure and strong is the harp's voice
> Wi' nane tae pluck a string.
>
> The harp utters the truth o' love,
> And tae a' the host that hears
> A thousand years are but as a day,
> And a day a thousand years.[48]

The poem's conclusion is devastatingly utopian in its outlook, for the "truth o' love" of which the harp sings dissolves the concerns of the immediate moment into an infinite time of artistic creation. In a sense, the harp is a trope for the poet's relation to historical tradition: singing against the demands of time, the harp is still made—quite materially— from the individual poet, who must always exist within time, vulnerable to its tyrannical authority.

But the triumph of art over time is always a Pyrrhic victory, as Adam knows so well. If Dinnerstein's feminist revision of Freud is appropriate to our understanding of these deceptively simple poems, so too is Herbert Marcuse's Marxist revision in *Eros and Civilization,* the product of another, rather different European sensibility transplanted to the postwar West Coast. In a pointed observation on the erotic impulse that sets the work of art against the power of time, Marcuse states that

Eros, penetrating into consciousness, is moved by remembrance; he uses memory in his effort to defeat time in a world dominated by time. But in so far as time retains its power over eros, happiness is essentially a thing of the *past.* . . . Time loses its power when remembrance redeems the past.

Still, this defeat of time is artistic and spurious; remembrance is no real weapon unless it is translated into historical action.[49]

The strengths and weaknesses of the consolation of Helen Adam's poetry may be found in this statement. The insistent desire to redeem the past idealistically, to rediscover in the Romantic tradition a source of contemporary poetic value, is unquestionably noble; and like all noble quests it bears within itself its doom. Adam's ballads are hardly "spurious" within themselves: their emotional as well as formal integrity challenge us to reconsider our conventional view of the changes that occur in literary (and hence social) history. We emerge from these poems as if awakening from a glamorous dream; our present concerns are suddenly conditional and even ephemeral compared to what we originally took to be the fairy tale stuff of antiquarians—if not children. Surely this is genuinely utopian matter; it bears a sense of plenitude to which we are almost invariably denied access.

Perhaps. For if the utopian is that which is always deferred, the "not yet," as Bloch himself identifies it, then we are confronted in this poetry with an act of redemption that has *not yet* been projected into the future: only by implication does the poem shape history into a continuum. Time is arrested as action ceases; in the end desire remains unfulfilled. And while unfulfilled desire in itself is a prerequisite for any utopian utterance (as in William Bronk's great poem "Unsatisfied Desire"), here the poem acts only by rehearsing its inability to act; and in this regard, it is as much a willful forgetting as it is a heroic remembrance. This accounts for the extraordinary stasis that informs many Adam's poems, a stasis that is the complement to their violently sensual surfaces.[50] Consider the poem "At Mortlake Manor":

> I fear, and I love, I love, and I fear,
> The Far Away Ladies now hovering near.
> I built a great house with a high garden wall,
> But the Far Away Ladies look over the wall.
>
> My wife says "I'll stay in the house where you dwell."
> The Far Away Ladies say always, "Farewell."
> They float past the windows, and smile as they pass.
> I beat with my hands on the sundering glass.
>
> My wife whispers "Yes," while the fire smoulders low.
> The Far Away Ladies sigh, "No" only "No."
> They mock the light flames of a mortal desire,
> Yet their's are the faces I see in the fire.
>
> My wife dreads the garden, so lonely, so dark,
> The sound of the river, the trees of the park.

The snakes in my garden are ancient and wise.
The Far Away Ladies look out of their eyes.

I fear, and I love, I love, and I hate,
The Far Away Ladies who follow my fate.
My wife is my dearest, from her I won't part.
But the Far Away Ladies o'er shadow my heart.[51]

Again we see the problematic nature of conventional domestic rela-
tionships, the lure of the uncanny and the wanton disinterestedness of
the supernatural as it possesses the speaker of the poem. The Far Away
Ladies are figures out of a nursery rhyme, and indeed, the speaker
sounds childish in his plight. But childishness barely hides the insidious
psychic peril presented here. Like the knight in Keats's "La Belle Dame
Sans Merci" (a precursor text to which Adam continually returns), the
victim here faces forces that "mock the light flame of a mortal desire."
Woman is either passive, familiar parlor temptation, or utterly weird,
unobtainable phantom; in either case sexual contact is forestalled, ener-
vated, and perverse. The speaker is unmanned, unable to possess him-
self, no less behave as the proper master of the house, his conventionally
prescribed role. The scenes are static tableaux in which desire seems
permanently arrested, and there hangs over all a morbidity that proves
more pleasurable than any act of fulfillment or consummation. The
poem is a closed circle in terms of its structure, and like a circle it has no
beginning or end: remembrance has reclaimed the past, but the poem
now consists of nothing but remembrance, brooding perpetually over a
past that becomes a monstrously eternal present.

The present, however, maintains its own special virtues, not the least
of which, as we observed in chapter 1, is its congruence with "the front,"
the point of greatest potential in time, no matter how much that poten-
tial appears to be denied. Despite the enervation that seems to permeate
Adam's lyrics, the degree of passion—libidinal, existential, social—ap-
pears at times to be inexhaustible, no matter how finely nuanced the
poem appears. One may read deeply of the dialectics of sex, class, and
age in Adam's "Goose Girl's Song," but regardless of how one situates the
text in historical, sociological, and psychological constellations, it remains
empowered by those poetic emotions that we are finally left to call
utopian:

My fingers smell of musk.
My breast is bright as fire.
My small face is faded
With the breath of desire.
I am a tree of lilac
In heavy summer bloom.

> I am the ache of summer
> And it's dull perfume.
>
> Oh! who will be my comfort?
> And crumble with his hands
> The flowery flesh that tires me,
> The blossom that demands.
> The white heavy blossom,
> The slowly swaying tree
> That shadows all the meadow
> Where once I walked free.[52]

Consider how this poem both broods over the past (the personal past of the speaker, "where once [she] walked free" and the literary past of the text, with its tropes recalling precursor poems such as "Ode to a Nightingale," "The Lotus Eaters," and "The Blessed Damozel") and anticipates the future (the speaker wonders "who will be my comfort," looking forward to that power which will free her from her longing body, which is also the "body" of the text). It is this simultaneously retrospective and anticipatory quality that opens and enriches the present moment of the poem, creating that extraordinary condition that Benjamin describes as "the Messianic cessation of happening."[53] The poem's present becomes an instance of the *Jetztzeit,* the time of the now, filled suddenly with unprecedented utopian or messianic possibility. Only such antithetical wisdom as this can break the spell of Helen Adam's poems.

I have come to that point in my study at which I can assert that while poems end—admit to closure—poetry as a continuum never does. If this statement appears simplistic, even in the light of such poetry as Duncan's and Helen Adam's, then I still have recourse to the work of that equally traditional poet, Ronald Johnson. No "West Coast" poet (though he now makes his home in San Francisco, he comes from Kansas and has traveled extensively), Johnson, with the support and encouragement of Duncan, has become the most adventuresome exponent of the synthetic, visionary attitude that has granted the San Francisco Renaissance, for all its quirks, access to some of the most stirring utopian utterance of our time. Johnson's lack of recognition (William Harmon, in his review of *Ark: The Foundations,* guesses that Johnson must have "fifty or so readers"[54]), may be due in part to that crucial distinction between poems and poetry that comes to the fore when his work, like that of Duncan, Pound, Olson or Zukofsky, is considered. As Guy Davenport says:

> These austere extremes of the poetic imagination are useful if difficult evocations, for Ronald Johnson's transmutation of the English poem reaches down to the very roots of poetry itself. If a poem has ever

occurred to Mr. Johnson, he has never written it down. At least he has
never published it. . . . If the finely textured geometry of words
Ronald Johnson builds on his pages is not what we ordinarily call a
poem, it is indisputably poetry.[55]

Poems are published by the thousand in literary magazines every year,
and most are eminently disposable. Poetry is a far rarer commodity. It
admits of no boundaries except those which necessity imposes upon it,
and even then determines the means by which its immanent bounty may
be further expressed. To use Johnson's phrase from *The Book of the Green
Man*, it is "A land, perpetually coming / to harvest."[56] This is, simply put,
the overriding theme in all of his poetry to date.

Such being the case, Johnson's poetry challenges the prevalent notions
of form and content, objectivity and subjectivity, despite its unques-
tionably traditional, even derivative orientation. Davenport again: "*Ob-
jective* and *subjective* are modes in the critic's mind; the poet scarcely
knows what they mean."[57] One one level, Johnson, even more than
Duncan, is a participant in the Grand Collage: he pointedly appropriates
an immense variety of sources in his text, allowing the reader to re-
discover relationships in art and nature that had previously been
obscured by preconceived, overly categorized modes of thought. These
sources are allowed to "speak for themselves" as objects in the text, but
the shaping subject speaks through them as well. *Radi os,* Johnson's
notorious "erasure" of *Paradise Lost,* is only the most extreme example of
this phenomenon: the extensive quotations in *The Book of the Green Man*
(for me, still the most wholly satisfying work) demonstrate how the
boundaries between author, reader and text consistently dissolve under
the pressure of the synthesizing imagination. Johnson's imagination,
which he conceives of as an extension of nature's procreative force,
continually quickens language, fertilizes it, resulting in the elaborate
word play especially prevalent in his most recent work. But even in his
early poetry, the link between natural forces and the poetic imagination
is quite explicit:

> Here—
>
> both lines of poetry, rows
> of trees,
> shall spring all
> seasons
> out 'of the lust of
>
> the earth,
> without
> a formal seed'.[58]

And in *The Book of the Green Man,* diction in itself is made to carry the burden of form and theme:

> From there up Wyndcliffe, wooded with huge oaks, where the eyes
> soar, like birds buoyed up in air:
>
> from the oak-tops—coral & willow with first leaf
> & tassle—to clusters of mistletoe
>
> & rookeries, down to gnarled boles slanting against wind
> & covered with growths
>
> of ivy, to the carpet of wood-anemone (wood-
> anemones, Flowers-Of-The-Wind),
>
> out, over the Wye turning through valleys of
> mists, 800 feet below.[59]

Proper syntax may not be found in this passage, but the organic movement of perception and thought that is prior to syntax surely may. More than any other contemporary poet, Johnson is dedicated to the ur-language of poetry. Thinking of Harry Partch, the American composer who also invents the instruments on which his music is to be played, Johnson declares

> that poems
> might be made as Harry Partch makes
> music, his instruments
> built by hand
>   —that we might determine our own
>
> intervals between
> objects,
>   as he constructs octaves
>
> of 43 tones.[60]

Johnson's attitude toward language demands of the critic not a fashionable deconstruction of the text, but rather its reconstruction, the careful appreciation of totality in which Duncan's poetry and Zukofsky's may instruct us as well. In one of his most carefully measured statements, Johnson reaffirms the older poets' conviction that lawful utterance is a natural as well as human phenomenon:

> Outside,
> between bone & page, circlings

of sap, stars, tide

hold meaning
as a nest holds speckled bird's eggs,

& I (like
Thoreau) sit here engrossed,

'between a microscopic & a telescopic
world',
attempting to read

the twigged, branchy writing

of frost, spider & galactic cluster. That the syllables!

—rock & flower & animal
alike—
among the words,

make Order.[61]

Johnson's emphasis on "syllables"—in nature and in language—is found in his rhythm, as the long and short lines, generously spaced, precisely articulate the studied enthusiasm of the poet-naturalist. Throughout his poetry, the music that results from such care may be as rough or as fluid as any landscape, but individual words are rooted in place, determined as much by their derivation or connotative power as by their denotative sense. Johnson's linguistic precision is inherited from the Objectivists: his fascination with lenses, with microscopic and and telescopic vistas, recalls the opening definition of Zukofsky's "An Objective": "The lens bringing the rays from an object to a focus."[62] Years before Ashbery writes his long-winded *Litany,* Johnson juxtaposes two sparely-made texts in "The Unfoldings" to indicate the simultaneous orders of the microscopic and telescopic views. Invoking Leeuwenhoek (inventor of the microscope), the astronomers Herschel and Kepler, the composers Janáček and Ives, Johnson answers Thoreau's question

'Who placed us with eyes
between a microscopic and a telescopic
world'?

thus

Janáčvek heard squirrels	Ives, in the 5th Symphony,

```
          screeching like this
                                   wrote the interlapping
                   clarinet.       counterpoint
   And saw night-birds stare       of

             into the strings      undulating lines
             of his piano.         of mountains
                                   with
                 Midges
             came from his         celestial
                                   orbits.
          woodwinds.63
```

As the poem continues, the texts again merge, turning about a central axis to demonstrate the movement

                                   Centripetal
                   Centrifugal:
                                   fugue, & petal.

But this is no gimmick, no coyly Postmodern trick: like Blake, Johnson demands that the text respond in its entirety to the linguistic perception of the universal order. Poetry is at once fugue and petal, the human ordering of cosmic impulses and the natural outgrowth of the mind's self-fertilization.

If this view of poetry seems too naively exalted, lacking in an awareness of specifically social conflicts, and potentially aligned to the ludic extravagance of much recent literary criticism, it is important to remind ourselves of the radical nature of Johnson's work—radical, again, as in roots. If Hugh Kenner is correct when he calls *Ark* religious poetry (on the volume's dust jacket), we must reply that religion and myth arise from humanity's crudest encounters with material phenomena, and consist in large part of its attempts to encode, organize, and comprehend those encounters on a communal level. Thus Johnson's sophisticated re-creation of the myth of the Green Man, for all its verbal elegance, takes us back through various historical levels of socialized ritual to a primitive wonder over the land's vegetative cycle and over human means to recapitulate that cycle in words. Even *Radi os* functions in terms of such rediscoveries, for what may be the seminal modern poem is treated as an archaeological site—yet another rich landscape—that, through patient delving, will yield previously submerged insight:

Shine inward, and
            there plant eyes
                        that I may see and tell

Of things invisible

                                        once

        thick as stars

The radiant image

                            the only
                            Garden[64]

The garden is to Johnson what the field is to Duncan or the "outside" is
to Spicer: a metaphysical locus for the expression of the utopian func-
tion of poetry. *The Book of the Green Man* begins its tour of rural Britain
with the poet standing in the garden of Wordsworth's Dove Cottage,
declaring his hopes for the poem:

        O
        let us give stems to
        the flowers!

        Substance to this
        fog: some

        subtle, yet enduring mold,

        a snare

        for bird-song,

        night, & rivers flowing.

        Let us catch
        the labyrinthine wind,
        in words—

        syllable, following
        on syllable,

        somewhere in these airs, these

        sinuous yews[65]

And by the end of the tour, at Shoreham, Johnson can affirm that

> It is here
> was Hesperides, *Paradisi in Sole*
> *Paradisus Terrestris.*
>
> I held a yellow twilight in my head.
> I saw the glow of its after-
> image, green & blue, circle the globes of apple.
> I walked upon the clods
> of cumulus, & saw a 'glory' moving always before me
> on the grass. And melody came, in openings
> of the air. All
> eyes. In Shoreham's Albion. A *Paradys*
>
> *Erthely.*[66]

As these passages should indicate, Johnson's engagement with the Romantic, visionary, and pastoral traditions in English poetry is both complexly mediated and startlingly immediate. Johnson has no qualms about displaying his erudition, and at his weakest (like his precursors) he is something of an ink-horn poet, a passionately pedantic collector and name-dropper. What saves *The Book of the Green Man* from its five densely printed pages of notes and references is the freshness of the language that Johnson appropriates, and the originality of the poetry that such an engagement produces. Coming to the British naturalists and poets from his apprenticeship with such Americans as Williams, Zukofsky, and Olson, Johnson understands how even the oldest textual materials may be approached with new eyes, as if they were objects to be discovered as he likewise discovers the mistletoe, ivy, and lichen that surround the oaks of the Lake District forests. For Johnson, the future lies dormant in the past, waiting to be awakened. Like the green world of rural England, and like the myth of the Green Man itself, poetry partakes in a potent, celebratory natural impulse; it regenerates itself out of precursor texts that have likewise been initiated into such knowledge. Johnson quotes Thoreau on the subject of old books, "as if they were making a humus for new literature to spring in," and confesses, "I lust after books with a certain 'Ohio soil', a rich silt of bibliography, books which lead to other books."[67]

What makes this more than a pleasantly quaint pastoral indulgence is Johnson's insistence on the intimate linkages of the subjective world of myth and poetry to the objective world of the empirical sciences; hence the authorities he cites are as often the old naturalists as they are the old poets. In an uncanny section of *The Book of the Green Man* called "Most Rich, Most Glittering, Most Strange," Johnson offers an elaborate list of

natural phenomena—some legendary, some real—that gradually co-
alesces into a hallucinatory litany of the human endeavor to comprehend
nature:

> Petrified Wood & Moss. Blood-
> stones, clumps of Amethyst, 'Isicles'.
> Curious stones from everywhere & several
> Humming-birds, with nests.
>
> Those opalescent clouds in the form
> of scales of fish: striped, undulating,
> cirrus-like—with spectral 'eyes'
> of a bright, metallic lustre.
>
> Fog-bow & Moon-bow. Haloes observed
> around the sun, with Mock Suns, upon days
> of peculiar, milky light. . . .[68]

Here Johnson attempts to demonstrate that the various spheres of
human activity are part of a single process: what fascinates the poet
likewise fascinates the scientist; the aesthetic spirit is one with the spirit
of scientific inquiry; and "vision" is a term common to both. The ecstatic
conclusion of *The Book of the Green Man* maintains its Objectivist exact-
itude, as the visionary light of Vaughan and Boehme yields to Johnson's
persistent love of the nominal world:

> *I walked up to the CLOUD,*
>
> *'a country*
> *where there is no*
> *night'*
>
> *but of moons*
> *& with heads of fish*
>
> *in the furrow,*
>
> *& on each*
> *ear, beneath a husk*
> *of twilight*
>
> *were as many suns as*
> *kernels*
>
> *& fields were far*
>
> *as the eye*
> *could reach.*

Then dipping their silver oars,

the eyes
shed characters of fire
in the grain,

its sheaves as if mackeral
shone on the waves

of air.[69]

Again Johnson combines the spiritual and the material, the microscopic and telescopic, but throughout, the language remains etched with studied precision, visually and musically compelling.

From such careful observation of even the most fantastic physical and mental events comes the dizzying structures of *Ark,* in which not the old naturalists but the contemporary physicists, astronomers, and biologists guide the poet's course. Arks (or arcs) traditionally betoken promises; and if the inchoate materials out of which Johnson is presently shaping his long poem seem especially hermetic or obscure, we should keep in mind that throughout his work, the process of shaping the poem has always been a crucial aspect of the poem itself. Thus, a promise is gradually made throughout the first volume, a promise to which Johnson has always been faithful:

"To do as Adam did"

through the twilight's fluoride glare Mercury in perihilion

(rotating exactly three times

while circling the sun twice)

to Pluto foot tilt up the slide at either plane

and build a Garden of the brain.[70]

Indeed, throughout his unique career, Johnson has implied his awareness of the poet's utopian calling. He has followed a course that is richly imbued with traditional attitudes, but in doing so, he has come to be regarded, like his precursors, as an avant-garde, even experimental poet. And he is. The impulse behind his work invariably creates a tension between conservation and invention that is manifested in the poet's shifting notions of form. What does not change, however, is the utopian conception of "Man"—and here, we may read in particular "the poet"—that Johnson gleans from Milton at the end of Book III of *Paradise Lost,* or "O III" of *Radi os:*

Worlds,
That both in him and all things,
                    drive
      deepest

                        Sun,

                    are all his works,

          created mind

                    Infinitude confined:

      quintessence

                    turned to star

                                Man; that light
          which else,

Still ending, still renewing,

                        is Paradise,
Adam's

          ecliptic,
                    in many an aery wheel[71]

Johnson's felicitous appropriation of Milton's "Infinitude confined" takes us to the furthermost reaches of the anagogic vision that inspires the poets under consideration in this chapter. The term "anagogic," of course, evokes Northrop Frye, whose definition of the anagogic phase of literary symbolism certainly enriches our understanding of these poets:

When we pass into anagogy, nature becomes, not the container, but the thing contained, and the archetypal universal symbols, the city, the garden, the quest, the marriage, are no longer the desirable forms that man constructs inside nature, but are themselves the forms of nature. Nature is now inside the mind of an infinite man who builds his cities out of the Milky Way. This is not reality, but it is the conceivable or

imaginative limits of desire, which is infinite, eternal, and hence apoc-
alyptic.[72]

A critical definition of this sort would at one time have served as a
sufficient conclusion to this discussion; and even now, the apocalyptic
pronouncements we have encountered here are brilliantly illuminated
by Frye's analysis. But in his Marxist revision of Frye's "Theory of
Symbols," Frederic Jameson observes that Frye reverses the original
medieval ordering of symbolic levels. The vision of community, which
was originally anagogic, is relegated to the subsidiary level of myth or
archetype, while Frye's version of the anagogic (quoted above) celebrates
the individual's "libidinal body." As Jameson explains:

> This terminological shift is thus a significant strategic and ideological
> move, in which political and collective imagery is transformed into a
> mere relay in some ultimately privatizing celebration of the category of
> individual experience. The essentially historical interpretive system of
> the church fathers has here been recontained, and its political ele-
> ments turned back into the merest figures for the Utopian realities of
> the individual subject.[73]

Indeed, of the poets we have considered here, only Duncan places great
faith in community; Helen Adam's notion of messianic empowerment,
from "Third Eye Shining," is more typical:

> Blindingly glorious
> The angels of the sun
> By their own ecstacy
> Round creation swung.
> Milleniums pass, their dance
> Is scarce begun.
> Hard are the shining hearts
> Of flames forever young.
> One center flame they love,
> I am that one.[74]

Here, the anagogic vision, beautiful as it is, reaches its ideological limits
in "the Utopian realities of the individual subject."
    The "recuperation" of either literature or literary criticism through a
negative hermeneutic such as this must inevitably generate the feeling of
Oedipal anxiety, and I am not at all sure that such anxiety is a coun-
terproductive force. If the parent text is somehow maimed through the
necessary procedures of demystification, then no amount of appreciative
exegesis will restore that lost aura of wholeness, the longing for which
should by no means be dismissed as mere nostalgia. Fortunately, literary
texts tend to resist sophisticated critical impositions: they implacably
reassert their resilience to ideological or linguistic reductionism, fore-

grounding their linguistic qualities when they are about to be reified into ideology, emphasizing their ideological content when they are about to be dissolved into a play of signs.

The poetry discussed here proves that this is the case, for it is self-conscious to the utmost degree. Verbal play consistently upsets reified patterns of belief throughout the work; strong assertions of belief suddenly settle linguistic indeterminancy. This is a poetry that continually reexamines and extends, changes and develops its primary sources of meaning. Unmindful of conventional generic restrictions—those of Postmodernism as well as prior literary discourses—the work of Duncan or Spicer or Helen Adam simultaneously defamiliarizes the lyric strategies of even the most contemporary poetry and restores the reader to a lost textual homeland "that is a place of first permission." But whether the poem returns to us its lyric bounty or denies us that plenitude we believed to be our own, its operations are circumscribed and accommodated by its utopian propensity, the anti-teleological telos to which, through suspicion or trust, it is wed.

And to be sure, this tendency survives and bears fruit. Johnson paid attention to Duncan (among others); the result is the growth of a new poetry that is, indeed, centered upon the process of its own growth. A somewhat younger poet, Ross Feld, paid attention to Spicer (among others); the result is the ghostly saying of his *Plum Poems* that is likewise a palpable growth. Duncan's meadow opens into Johnson's green wood; Spicer's lemon casts its shadow that is Feld's dark plum:

> A silence which settles the night
> unsettles me.
> It is not the absence of the yellow
> in one's bright eyes but
>
> a slight cooling in the head, sealing
> love to the sharp darkness.
> Out of that black, my name comes sailing
> in at me, chiffon and in
> someone else's voice, a
> soft pin put to me directly. "Ross"
> it says off the night. The voice says "Ross"
> like Hamlet's father. It falls from
> any cliff.
>
> At night you learn that you can't talk
> to yourself but only to Hamlet,
> to his father, to a cliff.[75]

For "Hamlet's father" read "Jack Spicer": the haunted becomes the haunter, the voice from the empty space of the future addressing the poet at the edge of his cliff.

The Utopia of Language

When Jack Spicer died in 1965, he was known mainly to a coterie of poets centered in the Bay Area. As I mentioned in the previous chapter, this remains true today, despite intermittent critical attention, special issues of various literary magazines, and even an MLA special session devoted to his work on the twentieth anniversary of his death. But although Spicer is still unknown to most readers of contemporary poetry, he proved to be remarkably prescient in his literary concerns and even the general evolution of his career from book to book. Recent concern over linguistic referentiality and the status of the speaking subject or "I" of the poem reminds us how painfully thorough Spicer was in addressing just these issues. Speaking of the current poetic "skepticism about language's ability to represent," poet and critic Michael Davidson observes that "the definitive remark on the subject was not made by a 'language poet' but by Jack Spicer in 1960: 'Where we are is in a sentence.' "[1]

Spicer insists upon the materiality of linguistic processes. For all his talk of spooks and Martians controlling utterance from some ostensibly metaphysical "outside," words in a Spicer poem can become vexingly tangible: "Strange, I had words for dinner / Stranger, I had words for dinner / Stranger, strange, do you believe me?"[2] Spicer makes us eat our words, not because they can provide physical sustenance, but because, after dining with the poet, we can no longer take the relationship of words to objects for granted. Our easy assumptions about referentiality are undermined with an insidious playfulness. It is strange to have words for dinner (Will we get up from the table as hungry as when we sat down?), and in this disruption of our verbal expectations, we become strangers to ourselves. The poem continues: "Honestly, I had your heart for supper / Honesty has had your heart for supper / Honesty honestly are your pain." Now we are no longer dining with the poet; rather, our heart, the seat of the emotions, the most intimate aspect of the self, is being devoured. We are no longer congruent with our inner being; we are divided from that which we assumed to be the truest part of our-selves. Not only is our sense of reality, as determined by language, cast into doubt by reading the poem, but in doing so, we are also proven false to ourselves. Yet, the voice of the poem protests the honesty of its actions; indeed, if the poem is to be trusted, honesty itself is what has eaten our heart and what has caused us such pain. Linguistic skepticism and a divided self—these are the existential terms we seem forced to accept. As the poem concludes, we are once again addressed: "Stranger, I had bones for dinner / Stranger, I had bones for dinner / Stranger, stranger, strange, did you believe me?" The poem has chewed us (and itself) to the bone.

The name of this poem is "Magic," and in considering recent Amer-ican poetry (that is, poetry from the late seventies through the early nineties), it seems to me that we are still very much under the same sort of spell that Spicer, among others, first unleashed. Critical generaliza-tions can never be congruent with literary practices, but in abstracting the theoretical problems with which poets have struggled during this period of time, critics (and sometimes poets themselves) often identify the two so clearly debated in Spicer's major work: the problems of referentiality and of the self. These problems add particular inflections to the concomitant issue with which most modern poets wrestle, that of historically appropriate form. As Davidson's remark indicates, this is especially true of the avant-garde writers associated with the movement known as language poetry.

The language poets represent an extension of but also a break from the linguistic, philosophical, and political assumptions that largely deter-mined the older styles of poetry discussed in previous chapters. Their lineage consists of writers who cast the integrity of the self into doubt by questioning referentiality and emphasizing the materiality of language; they frequently invoke such figures as Gertrude Stein, the Objectivists, Olson, Creeley, Spicer, and the Ashbery of *The Tennis Court Oath*.[3] At the same time, they have bolstered their work with references to Marx, Wittgenstein, the Russian Formalists, and the poststructuralists, marking them as the only group of contemporary poets willing to engage in an extensive theoretical consideration of the relationship of poetry to larger political, philosophical, and cultural issues. Indeed, part of the program of the language poets has been an invigorating challenge to traditional distinctions between verse and prose, literature and philosophy, aesthet-ics and politics, as well as to the institutions that maintain such distinc-tions. In a paradoxically self-promoting move, they have lambasted the academy, which has been all too eager to lionize them and admit some of them into its ranks. Such is the nature of modern avant-gardes in relation to modern universities. As Raymond Williams observes in his analysis of emergent practices to the dominant culture, "The alternative, especially in areas that impinge on significant areas of the dominant, is often seen as oppositional and, by pressure, often converted to it."[4] Language poetry, as an emergent writing practice, certainly offers an alternative to dominant modes, and often presents itself as oppositional. Whether this is truly the case remains to be seen, but I suspect that for all its subversive claims, language poetry is gradually (and happily) being absorbed by the university, the dominant institution which mediates nearly all literary activity in the latter part of our century.

Perhaps what is ultimately a more serious charge is that the theoretical work of the language poets is more lively and thought-provoking than their actual poems, which tend to be formulaic and constituted of a fairly predictable set of gestures—though perhaps no more predictable than any other period style in the history of verse. Tom Beckett raises this issue in an interview with Charles Bernstein, referring generally to the contributors to the journal $L=A=N=G=U=A=G=E$ as well as to Bernstein in particular. Bernstein replies by arguing that

> There is an annoying bait in this type of disassociative discrimination insofar as it's fueled by a valorization of the Poet who only writes Poetry (in the narrower sense of the verse tradition), since it is out of fear of this type of criticism, of being typed as a theoretician in mutual exclusion to being a Poet, that I think causes many poets to retreat from expressing themselves in modes other than verse, as if to include non-"poetic" subject matter or diction in one's writing taints the purity of the project. This view you suggest seems primarily a negation of the whole activity, *both*, perhaps out of a sense that it punctures the privileged domain of poetic discourse, and challenges the self-imposed limits of what the vocabulary and style of poetry are. So I would think the person who makes this point doesn't know *where* to find the poetry. Whatever "critical" writing I've done makes sense primarily in terms of the "poetry," is one and the same project.[5]

In this passage we can see both the strengths and the weaknesses of the position that Bernstein represents. Bernstein is right to attack the anti-intellectual prejudice against poets theorizing about their poetry, and one has only to reflect upon the history of English poetry to realize how many major poets produced essential critical statements as well. His insistence that dominant poetic conventions need not restrict the style or subject of the poem is also well-taken; likewise, we should honor his more personal claim that "It is inconceivable that what you are calling the theoretical essays could have developed without an active poetic practice."[6] But to what extent does this unity or reciprocity of poetry and theory affect our actual encounter with the poem? In what ways does the poem, without its theoretical corollaries, call upon us to read differently—and are we willing to be taught new ways of reading by this particular poem?

It would appear that Bernstein has not been careful enough in his discussion of the relationship between poetics and poetry, between theory and practice. This is understandable: for the poet-critic like Bernstein (and many of the other language poets), the two activities inevitably come to be regarded as part of a single project (though other poets take the route of writing a "poetics" through their practice alone). But for the reader, who may not be a critic or a poet, the relationship of the poem to its theoretical justification is secondary at best; theory is, as I just said, only a corollary to practice.[7] The reader puts poetry to the test, and as Zukofsky tells us, "The test of poetry is the range of pleasure it affords as sight, sound, and intellection. This is its purpose as art."[8] Language poetry, like all avant-garde writing, challenges the conventional means through which poetic pleasure is produced, variously manipulating the techniques of sight, sound, and intellection which constitute the poem. Through such manipulation, the boundaries of the poem could presumably be expanded indefinitely, accommodating whatever forms the avant-garde writer achieves. As Stevens says, "All poetry is experimental poetry."[9] Some experiments, however, are not as successful as others, regardless of how meticulously their procedures are described. But such judgments depend in turn on the reason that the experiments were conducted in the first place.

What language writing as a totalizing project asks of us, in effect, is a reevaluation of the notion of literary pleasure. The Modernist insistence on the difficulty of readerly pleasure appears relatively tame in the face of much of the language poets' work. In opposition to the modernism of a Zukofsky or a Stevens, language poetry no longer assumes that the Supreme Fiction must give "pleasure" at all, since "pleasure" is the dominant motivation and goal in the consumer society of late capitalism. As Jerome McGann observes, language poetry "does not propose for its immediate object pleasure, as Coleridge once said all poetry does. Its immediate objects are the illusions of pleasure."[10] In that most language poets are left-wing poststructuralists, this challenge makes perfect sense. After all, political conservatives have no qualms about referentiality, and certainly have no desire to question the unity of the (bourgeois) subject. These issues concern the language poets to such a great extent because they represent the most vulnerable of dominant cultural assumptions about the production and consumption of literature in a Postmodern capitalist society. If poetry continues to be read for pleasure, and if that pleasure is to endure through the most rigorous engagement with pressing historical circumstances, then the language poets are right to exploit these concerns in order to reorient our political experience of poetic gratification. But as Frederic Jameson says, if a specific pleasure "is to become genuinely political," then it "must always in one way or another also be able to stand as a figure for the transformation of social relations as a whole."[11] In other words, what is at issue here is language poetry's utopian propensity.

In order to appreciate the significance for contemporary poetry of these recently articulated matters, we must digress and consider the work of one of the most important Postmodern theorists, Michel Foucault. Let me stress that I do not consider Foucault to be a direct influence on language poetry as a movement or on any of the individual poets under discussion here, though many poets today, like other American intellectuals, have probably read him. Rather, I introduce him into this chapter not only because his theoretical concerns parallel the issues raised by some of the newer poets, but because his writing, despite its notorious elusiveness, can provide a clear site for an ideological analysis of these issues. Foucault's notions of referentiality and the authorial subject lead us to what I call the utopia of language, a hypostatized attitude toward language which is equally the product of ideological and utopian thought. On the one hand, Foucault sees linguistic practices as one of the prime means through which repressive power, often in the form of the rapacious "will to truth," is maintained in a given social structure. On the other hand, language, or to use Foucault's more socially inflected term, discourse, is discovered to have a special virtue: it can open a utopian space in normative social relations where reference and self are blissfully destabilized. This utopian attitude toward language itself, regardless of the particular techniques through which language is deployed, links Foucault's theories with the conditions of recent American poetry.

I would really like to have slipped imperceptibly into this lecture, as into all the others I shall be delivering, perhaps over the years ahead. I would have preferred to be enveloped in words, borne way beyond all possible beginnings. At the moment of speaking, I would like to have perceived a nameless voice, long preceding me, leaving me merely to enmesh myself in it, taking up its cadence, and to lodge myself, when no one was looking, in its interstices as if it had paused an instant, in suspense, to beckon to me. There would have been no beginnings: instead, speech would proceed from me, while I stood in its path—a slender gap—the point of its possible disappearance.[12]

So begins "The Discourse on Language," one of Foucault's most important essays, and the one in which his vision of language's utopian possibilities is most patent. In order to counteract the power of an introduction or point of initiation, Foucault expresses his desire to "slip imperceptibly" into a beckoning stream of language which exists prior to his individual utterance. This strangely childlike wish "to be enveloped in words" indicates Foucault's view of the innocence of language in a state of pure duration and infinite accessibility, distinct from language's appropriation by institutions, which "solemnise beginnings" and "impose ritual forms upon them."[13] Institutions are threatened by the boundless expressivity of language; hence, "in every society the production of discourse is at once controlled, selected, organised and redistributed according to a certain number of procedures, whose role is to avert its powers and dangers, to cope with chance events, to evade its ponderous, awesome materiality."[14] The "will to truth" fixes reference and seeks power over the polysemous nature of language, hoping "to master and control the great proliferation of discourse, in such a way as to relieve its richness of its most dangerous elements."[15]

Prior to an actual analysis, which must inevitably betray the speaker's own will to truth, and in place of a ritualized beginning, Foucault's utopia stands forth, only to be glimpsed throughout the body of the ensuing text. It lies "on the other side of discourse," in a space beyond the institutional appropriations of language. Free of the textual hierarchies and dividing practices always imposed upon language, liberated from the will to truth, it is, as Foucault says of Borges's linguistic play, "a lyrical dream of talk reborn, utterly afresh and innocent, at each point; continually reborn in all its vigour, stimulated by things, feelings or thoughts."[16] Yet this notion of language as endlessly renewable and instantaneously responsive can only be a dream, can only be a utopian construct (as Foucault remarks elsewhere, "utopias permit fables and discourse: they run with the very grain of language"[17]). In reality, "True discourse, liberated by the nature of its form from desire and power, is incapable of recognising the will to truth which pervades it; and the will to truth, having imposed itself upon us for so long, is such that the truth it seeks to reveal cannot fail to mask it."[18] Thus, discourse, which in its "true" (that is, its ideal) state would be innocent of desire and power, is in its actual state complicitous in the machinations of our will to truth. Power, always the key term in Foucault's work, in this instance has corrupted some pristine condition of language that we can only begin to perceive. In what amounts to its fallen state, language has become an instrument bound up in the exercise of power: "We must conceive discourse as a violence that we do to things, or, at all events, as a practice we impose upon them."[19] Because of Foucault's obsessive concern with power, language, which in its referential aspect is our means of explaining and hence mastering our world, becomes nothing less than organized violence.

This dialectic of ideology and utopia, which obtains in Foucault's thinking about language, is equally applicable to his theory of the authorial subject: the more he denies the primacy of the authorial subject, the more utopian his theorizing becomes. Longing to amplify "the stirring of an indifference" as it poses Samuel Beckett's crucial question—

"What difference does it make who is speaking?"—Foucault invokes the threat of endlessly proliferating speech in the face of authorial and institutional strictures.[20] Against the prevailing order of things, replete with its linguistic powers of exclusion and of centralizing authority, he sets the free circulation of discourse, envisioned in all of its blissful anonymity.

In "What Is an Author?" as well as "The Discourse on Language," Foucault *assumes* the death of the author as unified subject, while at the same time vigorously exercising his formidable rhetorical skills in order to excavate that by now common "space into which the writing subject constantly disappears."[21] Foucault's need to perform an autopsy upon the author, which results in his brilliant deconstruction of the writing subject into a dispersed, anatomized "author-function," reveals a basic anxiety on his part: Will the author stay dead? At various points in his analyses, Foucault concedes that this will not be the case. The subject should not be entirely abandoned; rather, "one must return to this question, not in order to reestablish the theme of an originating subject, but to grasp the subject's points of insertion, modes of functioning, and system of dependencies."[22] Like Jacques Derrida, who claims not to "destroy" the subject but to "situate it,"[23] Foucault denies the author its originating power while still maintaining its identity in the general discursive system. However, both the author's identity and the discursive system are historically relative terms; the author-function, as Foucault defines it, materializes through a rigorous investigation of historical difference. Thus, individuals may *resume* the functions of the author, but discourse itself always precedes and to a great extent constitutes the subjective writing act.

Foucault is not unaware of the problem in affording discourse a privileged position over the autonomous writing subject: "Giving writing a primal status seems to be a way of retranslating, in transcendental terms, both the theological affirmation of its sacred character and the critical affirmation of its creative character."[24] Here, Foucault tacitly acknowledges the endless regress or "bad infinity" faced by theorists when they attempt to trace utterance back to its ontological ground. As Derrida might say, utterance "always already" posits an originating subject, even when the individual has been displaced by a utopian vision of the discursive system itself. While the identification of Foucault's utopia of language does not necessarily cast his deconstruction of referentiality and the author into doubt, it does adumbrate the ideological limits of Foucault's theories.

As we have noted throughout this book, one of the most important aspects of utopian thought as embodied in any given text is that, as Ernst Bloch says, it "persists through the ages, once the social basis and ideology of an epoch have decayed." Such being the case, the relativistic historicism of Foucault's project ultimately may founder against the irreducible metaphysic of subjective desire. Utopian yearning, even when posited in the free play of subjectless discourse, still requires a subject from which such yearning may originate—and no more eloquent author of this yearning may be found than Foucault himself. Furthermore, the fact that Foucault must perform his acts of deconstruction in the "presence" of a utopian goal confirms the largely unresolved ideological conflict to be found in all such Postmodern attacks on the subject, whether they are found in critical theory, or, as we shall see, in poetry. Defending the notion of the subject against such attacks, Olivier Revault d'Allonnes argues that

> these philosophers, claiming to be modern, proclaimed the death of the subject and the end of humanism, thus accomplishing the final murder that the dominant ideology itself dare not perpetrate. By disposing of the last rights of the subject in a world which repents of having given the subject too many as it is, one becomes not merely the accomplice but a constituent element of the system.[25]

Perhaps it is Foucault's clinging to a vestige of utopian potential posited in language itself, and not his corrosive interrogations of our will to truth in all its anatomized variations, that may prove his most important contribution to our understanding of the writing subject within a discursive system.

The utopian potential of "talk reborn," appealing to the aesthetic and political sensibilities of the Postmodern writer, is to be found in the work of the language poets to the same extent as in the work of Foucault. In making this assertion, however, I must again invoke the vexed distinction between literary theory and practice, one that I feel is necessary to maintain. As we have seen in Foucault, the theoretical dream of a language beyond language, beyond what we do with and to language, becomes a horizon line, a glimmering boundary at the furthest edge of expository prose. In the impossible delight of passing that boundary, the violence of referentiality would be cleansed, the proliferating bounty of words would be reclaimed, and the self, long sickened with the thrill of discursive power, would be stripped of authority so that it may celebrate its indifference.

But what does it mean to really move toward this horizon, rather than merely speculate about it? What happens to literary language and to the speaking subject of the text? According to Charles Bernstein, the result would be

> Not "death" of the referent—rather a recharged use of the multivalent referential vectors that any word has, how words in combination tone

and modify the associations made for each of them, how "reference" then is not a one-on-one relation to an "object" but a perceptual dimension that closes in to pinpoint, nail down (*this* word), sputters omnitropically (the in in the which of who where what wells), refuses the build up of image track/projection while, pointillistically, fixing a reference at each turn (fills vats ago lodges spire), or, that much rarer case . . . in which reference, deprived of its autonomous reflex reaction of word/stimulus image/response roams over the range of associations suggested by the word, word shooting off referential vectors like the energy field in a Kirillian photograph.[26]

The lively, darting tone here, certainly an attempt at the recharging of language to which Bernstein aspires, seems rather remote from Foucault's sibylline murmur, with its undercurrents of longing. Yet, in both instances, the desideratum is a heightened sense of discursive freedom, a renewal of language's generative, polysemous, "multivalent" potential. Likewise, in an often cited discussion that is obviously informed by Foucault, Bernstein argues that

> It's a mistake, I think, to posit the self as the primary organizing feature of writing. As many others have pointed out, a poem exists in a matrix of social and historical relations that are more significant to the formation of an individual text than any personal qualities of the life or voice of an author. I do not wish to discuss the well-known position about the "death of the author"; but there is no question that authorship is a concept that has been given much more significance than it merits, and as such is an obstacle for reading and writing to overcome; even though I do not feel that it makes sense to carry these views to the extreme of cancelling authorship as a factor completely, making a text exclusively the product of a discourse or a period, since in crucial ways a poem is as much a resistance as a product, and for the moment at least the individual is the most salient concept with which to describe the site of resistance.[27]

Just as Foucault insists on analyzing rather than merely refuting the role of the author function in discursive systems, so Bernstein recognizes the need to maintain authorship as an operative category in the reading and writing processes. His rationale is primarily political: If the poem is to function as a "resistance" rather than as a "product," then the notion of individuality must be maintained at least "for the moment" under prevailing historical conditions. This position resembles that of another recent theorist of textual subjectivity, Paul Smith:

> What is at stake here is a sense of how and under what conditions subject/individuals simultaneously exist within and make purposive intervention into social formations. Such intervention can and does take place, actively or passively, through single people or collectives,

privately and publicly. It can take the form of a refusal as much as an intervention; it can be in the service of conservatism as much as of disruption. It may well call upon an experience of class; but more generally it calls upon the subject/individual's history. . . .[28]

Smith's "intervention," like Bernstein's "resistance," posits the subject as an enduring agent of struggle against the dominant culture, though Smith specifically notes that such agents of intervention may range across the ideological spectrum. Yet in both cases, the individual maintains a degree of integrity which is associated with the utopian propensity of a given action.

But if that action is the composition of a poem, then Bernstein remains ambivalent: "The valorization of the author function, in its current guises as voice, persona, autobiography, and self-expression, hierarchializes a complicated constellation of variables including structure, social context, genre, method, politics."[29] The subordination of self-expression to these other poetic variables seems reasonable enough, especially in the light of the worst excesses of the confessionals or those poets of the seventies whose work becomes, as Charles Altieri puts it, "a psychological hot tub."[30] In Bernstein's most intriguing poems, the self remains a flickering presence of compelling power.

In his essay on language poetry, Jerome McGann calls Bernstein's "For Love Has Such a Spirit That If It Is Portrayed It Dies" a "Shelleyan performance" and praises its shifting "forms of order" and its typically "antinarrative" stance.[31] The first part of the poem is indeed produced under conditions of great semantic and grammatical disperson, so that the direct expression of personal feelings which one expects of the lyric I of the traditional love poem is continually thwarted:

> . . . Aims departing after one another
> & you just steps away, listening,
> listless. Alright, always—riches
> of that uncomplicated promise. Who—what—.
> That this reassurance (announcement)
> & terribly prompted—almost,
> although. Although censorious and even more
> careless. Lyrical mysticism—harbor, departing
> windows. For love I would—deft equator.[32]

Here certain phrases associated with love ("you just steps away," "that uncomplicated promise," "lyrical mysticism") are interrupted or broken off before the emotion can be fully portrayed: surely a subversion of the self as the primary organizing feature of the poem. Even Robert Creeley, whom Bernstein admires, is implicitly criticized for his plain expression of feeling by the phrase "For love I would—deft equator," a disruption of the first lines of Creeley's "The Warning" ("For love—I would / split open your head").

But what makes this poem more than a pyrotechnic display of words "shooting off referential vectors" is the way that the lyric I reasserts itself about halfway through the text. As we noted earlier, language poets admire Jack Spicer for the ghostly voices which disturb personal utterance in many of his books. In Bernstein's poem, just the opposite occurs, as out of the cacophony a relatively stable voice begins to speak, and quite movingly at that:

> This darkness, how richer than a moat it lies. And
> my love, who takes my hand, now, to watch all this
> pass by, has only care, she and I. We deceive
> ourselves in this matter because we are in
> the habit of thinking the leaves will fall or
> that there are few ways of breaking the circuit.
> How much the stronger we would have been had
> not—but it is something when one is lonely
> and miserable to imagine history on your side. On
> the stoop, by the door ledge, we stand here, coffee
> in hand. . . .[33]

The anomie of the voice confirms a surprisingly Romantic notion: that the failure of personal relations betokens a general historical impasse, a sense of lost opportunities and regret "that there are few ways of breaking the circuit." Appropriately enough, the bittersweet feeling of regret in these lines is reminiscent of Ashbery at his most humane, as in "Street Musicians" or "As One Put Drunk into the Packet Boat." The sheer wistfulness of Bernstein's broken sentence, "How much stronger we would have been had/not—," while it does not altogether negate his programmatic distrust of the self, certainly casts his attitude in a more ambiguous light.

That same ambiguity is reflected in "Looking About," a poem which is otherwise quite different from "For Love Has Such a Spirit" in terms of tone and emotional register. If the latter sounds like Ashbery, the former hearkens back to the Objectivists:

> How many times sat here same spot
>   and wondered in this way, going
>   down to this place, having things and
>   doing things, all of whom
>   wave goodbye when you get too close.
>   For instance, today I was at,
> now all of a sudden feel, but
>   what think of turning the benches,
>   loosening things. A

cycle comes and a cycle comes wheeling around,
how loosen it,
    how is it fastened inside. I
        like to think of the time
      I lost wasting for trains in the
            subway. . . .[34]

The Objectivist orientation of these lines accounts, at least partly, for the diffuse sense of the "I" in its act of "looking about." The Objectivists' desire to make the poem an act of engagement with external phenomena necessitates a radical repositioning of traditional poetic subjectivity: as we have seen, both the sincerity or truth of the subject and the achievement or perfection of the poem depend not on degree of "self-expression" but on the measure of the writing as it is fit to the contours of objective reality. As Zukofsky says, "Writing occurs which is the detail, not mirage, of seeing, of thinking with the things as they exist, and of directing them along a line of melody. Shapes suggest themselves, and the mind senses and receives awareness."[35]

A good deal of Objectivist poetry is occupied with "thinking with the things as they exist"; both the form and content of the poem stem from such focused acts of perception as they occur one after another. Writing tracks and reveals reality, but paradoxically, it makes reality as well. Consider these lines from Zukofsky's "Chloride of Lime and Charcoal":

        The dog in the third story
        Brownstone window looks
        Down into the street
        Left and right
        Much like his master
        Distracted
        To see
        What is going
        On in the world.

        Is the skyline still there
        Are the buildings
        A new bridge
        Or the new ramp?
        Philosophy moves
        Faster than sound
        To what purpose?[36]

The dog and his master look out of the window "To see / What is going / On in the world": simple being in a state of what Hegel would call sense-certainty is moved to encounter external phenomena. Perception leads to speech, and through the linguistic process of interrogation, objects are named: "buildings," "a new bridge," "the new ramp." This process brings objects to consciousness, confirms their existence, but simultaneously calls them into question. Ultimately, the dog is not like his master: the self-conscious human being philosophizes; through the medium of language, thought moves even faster than perception, though there are times when we may wish it otherwise.

Bernstein's "Looking About" takes Zukofsky's Objectivist project further. In the passage from "Chloride of Lime and Charcoal," the voice of the poem shifts almost imperceptibly between third-person and first-person (or at least a free, indirect style indicating first-person), stationing the reader both outside and inside the dog and his master as they look at the world. We are aware of the self observing itself as it observes external phenomena. In "Looking About," the use of the first-person is more thorough. The perceiving "I," scanning its surroundings, moves fluidly through the medium of language as sense impressions continually register on consciousness as simple words. Unlike other Bernstein poems which employ (sometimes in a fairly labored way) exotic or specialized vocabularies, carefully engineered structural techniques, and jarring disruptions of syntax, this poem comes close to that idealized murmur of language itself, which, in Foucault's dream, precedes and enmeshes all speech-acts. Here, language speaks the speaker who, while not entirely passive in his wondering state, is completely susceptible to the play of words. "I / like to think of the time / I lost wasting for trains in the / subway." The slip between the expected "waiting" and the actual "wasting" indicates how we are meant to understand that language, and not the speaking subject, is in control. As is said later in the poem:

> I just flow out the rhythm,
> clip to temptation, pattern
> that back, ie physical, of thought, me
> on the way out of, the other side
> of. . . .[37]

Patterns of thought and language, the interplay of physical and mental processes, supersede the "I," which simply flows along with the sensuous rhythm of the text.

The free expression of these patterns, an act that includes but can hardly be said to originate from the individual subject, constitutes what Bernstein calls "the syntax of the heart." This phrase comes from a strange allegory, "The Only Utopia Is in a Now," a piece in which Bernstein lampoons those who regard writing such as his as antiemotional and stiflingly intellectual. Writing a dialectical prose that reads like a slyly updated version of *The Marriage of Heaven and Hell* (Blake is actually quoted at one point), Bernstein both criticizes false notions of Utopia and defends his own vision of linguistic freedom. Taking a lesson from modern dystopian writers (Kafka, Orwell, and Huxley come to mind), Bernstein combines Romanticism with a critique of the "topsy-turvy" world of ideological language control.

As the piece opens, a group of "those without any names in the story" arrive at a sign saying "Utopia," though one of the group "who could read subtexts" quickly reveals that "'Utopia' was inscribed in such a way as to cover over the words 'private property.'" Another in the group "who could read pretexts" sees that the sign says "Holier than thou." Suddenly threatened by an enraged man who regards the group as "unemotional," they seek an explanation for their predicament.[38] A sympathetic woman who, in speaking to them, gradually emits beams of visionary light, reveals that in this "Utopia,"

> what is called "thinking" is absolutely forbidden in the name of what is called "emotion." You're only supposed to write and say what everyone else knows, and to write and say it in the way everyone else has already heard it. In fact, they issue a manual, *Acceptable Words and Word Combinations* and everyone talks and writes only in permutations derived from this book. It's no use arguing, since anyone who disagrees is called anti-emotional and, regardless of their gender, is also called "male." This is what makes everything so topsy-turvy. You see, emotion doesn't express itself only in words we already know. But people here who talk about emotion don't really want to experience it, they only want simulations of it in patterns of words they've already heard. In other words, they only want to hear what they already know, and they call this repetition, which is after all somewhat comforting, "emotion."[39]

This passage seems to have as its inspiration the slogans of two Modernist programs: Pound's urging writers to "Make It New," and Viktor Shklovsky's understanding of literary technique as a "making strange" *(ostranenie)* or defamiliarization of language. As an advocate for the constant renovation of language through experimentation, Bernstein understandably links stale, repetitive language with a false sense of comfort and an aggressive anti-intellectualism. Without linguistic experimentation that reveals new patterns and the expression of genuine emotion, we become victims of kitsch. Any preconceived notion of proper linguistic use can only result in totalitarianism: like the functionaries creating Newspeak in *1984*, the inhabitants of Bernstein's "Utopia" can only write and speak according to their manual, *Acceptable Words and Word Combinations*. Thus the only (true) utopia is in a now, when immediate social and linguistic exigencies spontaneously combine to produce the syntax of the heart. This is the message at the piece's conclusion, rhapsodic, but with an undertone of gentle mockery:

> When we hear the syntax of the heart, in words that may well seem new and strange to ears trained only to understand the old and familiar, we commune with the oneness of us-all that is our communal body, language. Don't be afraid, gentle writers, gentle speakers, that you won't communicate or will be too intellectual. Only when such concerns fall away, like calluses from our tongues, and we are left just to do and be, not trying to communicate out of a fear of being unable to, will language take its rightful place as love.[40]

Only through the defamiliarization of its utterance can emotion be acknowledged as genuine—but who remains to witness this virtually apocalyptic change? For in the communal body that is both language and love, where reference takes on a new immediacy, the self dissolves in universal linguistic bliss.

Yet what is experienced on the inside as bliss may be endured on the outside as boredom. Reading, as I have implied, is different from writing insofar as the reading self in its ineluctable search for meaning and pleasure (or perhaps meaning *as* pleasure) longs to encounter an other which it can gradually know in the contours of the other's alternative subjectivity. In order for a work of literature to be more than a consumable commodity ("culinary" literature, as Hans Robert Jauss puts it), it must undermine reader expectations. There is no better way to accomplish this than to thwart that search for the subjectivity of an other by defamiliarizing the referent and continually repositioning the voices of the text. But the risk involved in this strategy may be just as serious as that involved in simply following the accepted conventions of a given genre: whereas in the latter case, the text may be consumed as a mere entertainment, in the former case, the text may be rejected as offering too little that gratifies the reader's desire to encounter an alternative subjectivity. Whether the writer's goal regarding his or her audience is social transformation or formal accomplishment (and, of course, these are not mutually exclusive), endless defamiliarization may prove as ineffectual as strict adherence to the standards of a generic status quo.

Language poets succeed when they resist the temptation to push their avant-garde strategies to the limit. We usually think of groundbreaking literature as extremist in some dimension, but in this case, the formal extremism of the writing is such that the work frequently is hurled back on itself, inadvertently producing an obscurantism that goes against the express intentions of the writer. In "Disappearance of the Word, Appearance of the World," one of the most important (and explicitly Marxist) documents of the movement, Ron Silliman explains that

> What happens when a language moves toward and passes into a capitalist stage of development is an anaesthetic transformation of the

perceived tangibility of the word, with corresponding increases in its expository, descriptive and narrative capacities, preconditions for the invention of "realism," the illusion of reality in capitalist thought. These developments are tied directly to the function of reference in language, which under capitalism is transformed, narrowed into referentiality.[41]

For Silliman, the politically engaged writer attempts to reverse this "anaesthetic transformation" by "placing the issue of language, the repressed signifier, at the center of the program" and "placing the program into the context of conscious class struggle."[42]

The irony here is that Silliman's own writing focuses on the previously repressed signifier to such an extent that its expository, descriptive, and narrative capacities are almost totally lost. In *Tjanting*, his book-length prose work, a transformation takes place that is every bit as "anaesthetic" as that which ostensibly occurs to language in a "capitalist stage of development." What begins as an interesting experiment in self-deconstructing personal narrative becomes an increasingly disjointed barrage of sentences:

> My shadow on the off-white wall is writing. Slippery elm throat lozenge. Cat chooses to sit atop flat old brown paper bag. Fine pharmaceuticals since blah blah. Utter filth verb noun someone to clean up mouse parts cat puke. His eyes burnd right into his skull smell of tobacco in hair & shirt. Modular stool drop. By now familiar territory. Need to make do. Prisms' little rainbows on wall till clouds loom up. Nothing to do with the previous thing. Active ingredients.[43]

Granted, there is a certain exuberance here, a delight in the heterogeneity of contemporary discourse. And Marjorie Perloff is right to note, in her comparison of a passage from *Tjanting* to a sentimental reminiscence in a poem by Galway Kinnell, that Silliman's work usefully counters an obsessive concern with the uniqueness of personal experience with a more self-conscious "familiarity with literary codes" instead.[44] But what Perloff does not note is that while readers are at first sensitized to the play of the signfier in *Tjanting*, they gradually succumb to the obsessive sameness of the technique. Although many of Silliman's sentences could be identified as minute descriptions of the author's day-to-day existence, their random intermingling with sentences based on a wide variety of other codes finally results in the work's numbing style. The utopian murmur of language turns out to be an interminable, affectless chat.

This is not to single out Silliman for harsh criticism. Like most of the writers identified with language poetry, he combines leftist ideology, poststructuralist theory, and an avant-garde posture in a simultaneous effort to politicize art and aestheticize politics. The result is not a new, alternative notion of "realism," as is claimed for these writers' work (often by and in support of each other), but a fin-de-siècle style as rarefied as that of any pre-Raphaelite or Symbolist. Late nineteenth-century aestheticism gives us an ecstatically cloying literature in which spirit and flesh, death and beauty, are proven to be one and the same. Late twentieth-century aestheticism gives us a literature in which, all such binary oppositions having been deconstructed, language finally absorbs and nullifies reality while claiming to enact it and give it new life.[45]

Yet the methods as well as the theoretical underpinning of language poetry cannot be dismissed. Perhaps the time has come to see past both the self-promotion and the oppositional gestures of this latest avant-garde. As T. S. Eliot says, speaking of the role played by groups of relatively young or unknown writers "with certain affinities or regional sympathies between them":

> Such groups frequently bind themselves together by formulating a set of principles or rules, to which usually nobody adheres; in course of time the group disintegrates, the feebler members vanish, and the stronger ones develop more individual styles. But the group, and the group anthology, serve a useful purpose: young poets do not ordinarily get, and indeed are better without, much attention from the general public, but they need the support and criticism of each other, and of a few other people.[46]

The language poets are no longer young; they have produced a number of group anthologies (such as Silliman's *In the American Tree* and Douglas Messerli's *"Language" Poetries*); and at this point the strongest among them are indeed developing more individual styles. These writers would best be served through focusing critical attention on them as individuals, still keeping in mind the principles and affinities that led to the formation of their group identity and reputation. I am aware that in calling for greater scrutiny of the work through the lens of the individual writer, I am violating an article of faith shared by poststructuralist theorists and the language poets themselves: that criticism should question, if not explode, what was once, in Foucault's words, "the solid and fundamental unit of the author and the work."[47] The taboo against the author as a fundamental unit of criticism has, in the case of the language poets, successfully concentrated attention instead on the political principles of an alternative literary collectivity and on the formal principles of an alternative notion of poetic language. But the extent to which these principles operate in a number of increasingly mature and distinct (though still related) personal styles remains to be explored.

To conclude this chapter, I would like to analyze two poems in order to demonstrate how the principles at work in language writing play an important role in the situation of poetry at the present time. The first of these poems in Robert Hass's "The Image," from *Praise;* the second is Michael Palmer's response, which appears in section 12 of *Notes for Echo Lake,* a long poem which is interspersed among other texts in Palmer's volume by the same name. *Notes for Echo Lake* 12 is subtitled "disorders of the song," and the ninth poem in that section, marked "for R.H.," is precisely that: a "disordering" of Hass's original poem, so that certain ideas about referentiality and the self implicit in the text, but neglected or even repressed by Hass himself, can emerge and be recognized. Palmer's text defamiliarizes the linguistic assumptions in Hass's beautiful but more conventional poem, so that when read together, the two create a verbal and thematic counterpoint or dialectic. This utopian refunctioning of prevailing linguistic conditions attests to the strengths still to be found in recent American poetry.

Widely acknowledged as one of the most talented poets now in midcareer, Robert Hass has yet to be defined precisely in terms of the various tendencies in contemporary poetry, and in the main that is to the good. Charles Altieri is his best critic; he considers *Praise* as an example of what he terms the scenic style, but regards this volume as a more intelligent and self-conscious variant of a mode that can quickly become simplistic in its attempts at sincerity and "natural" expression. For Altieri,

> Hass is our best example of rhetoric employed as sincerity. But it will not do to treat rhetoric in his work as primarily the means for creating complex apprehensions. Hass is at least as interested in the powers that work through the process of apprehending as he is in the specific understanding of an experience he achieves. That is why his best poems are so fluid. Poetic style is inseparable from personal style, and the complexity of person depends on not allowing any single attitude to congeal into lyric self-congratulation. The person takes form in and as the voice capable of integrating a variety of lyric moments.[48]

Hass is always skeptical of the way he positions the lyric "I" in his poems, and his moving descriptions of the natural world often expand outward with equal skepticism into more abstract statements of remembrance, desire, and loss. Strongly impressed by the poststructuralist psychology of Jacques Lacan, Hass has taken to heart the idea

> that the resolution of the Oedipus complex and the acquisition of language occurred around the same time, they were the same thing. The *non* of you-can't have-your-mother and the *nom* of the father and his access to mastery of the world through symbols were identical, so that the laws of language were the very form of consciousness and they carried its freight of loss and guilt and symbolic power.[49]

This explanation of Lacan's main premises appears in Hass's essay on Robert Creeley, as Hass drives toward a discussion of Creeley's radical displacements of the "I." But Hass's understanding of Lacan is as important to his own poetry as it is to Creeley's. Thus, for me, Hass is at his best when he works within and against the scenic style, that is, when he strains away from landscape and from details of the physical world entirely to reach a fluid inner world filled with greater psychic risks, greater threats to rhetorical integrity, but even more resonant language. Ironically, a Lacanian sense of psycho-linguistic doubt and loss strengthens Hass, and his most successful poems in *Praise* become remarkably skillful mediations between the security of the object world and the instability of all verbal making.

This leads us to "The Image":

> The child brought blue clay from the creek
> and the woman made two figures: a lady and a deer.
> At that season deer came down from the mountain
> and fed quietly in the redwood canyons.
> The woman and the child regarded the figure of the lady,
> the crude roundnesses, the grace, the coloring like shadow.
> They were not sure where she came from,
> except the child's fetching and the woman's hands
> and the lead-blue clay of the creek
> where the deer sometimes showed themselves at sundown.[50]

Unlike some of Hass's longer and more linguistically self-conscious poems (such as "Heroic Simile," "Meditation at Lagunitas," and "Like Three Fair Branches from One Root Deriv'd"), "The Image" betrays a powerful wish for a magically simple, direct relation between creative activity and the natural world. Psychologically, the poem presents a preoedipal dyad of mother and child, without the anxious presence of the father and his symbolic order. Out of the primal matter of earth and water, the mother ritually fashions two little idols or images for herself and the child. The figure of the deer connects them to the grace of being which they observe around them, while the figure of the woman represents the mother herself, who in turn connects the world of human activity to the world of nature, of the mother-goddess. A sense of mystery pervades the gestures of the poem, and the stillness of some imaginary, prehistoric time before language. In the primal matrix of "the image," object calls to object and is immediately answered, with none of the endless, intervening distances of linguistic self-consciousness.

It is just this awareness that Michael Palmer seeks to recall by using Hass's poem as the basis of his own. Indeed, one of the primary aims of all of Palmer's work is to return us to this awareness. In this respect,

Palmer may be considered a language poet, and in regard to the crucial issues of reference and the self, his attitude is very close to that of the other poets we have considered under that rubric. Yet Palmer has also distanced himself from the group most often associated with the term "language poetry," and as I have argued elsewhere, his work, concerned with what he calls "the mystery of how words refer," connects him to various mystical, hermetic, and Romantic traditions as well.[51] A case could be made for Palmer occupying a middle ground between poets like Hass and Bernstein: like Hass, Palmer maintains a highly ritualized sense of the text, but like Bernstein, he strategically resists normative conventions of reference and the lyric "I." Often, the result is a poem which ritualistically questions its own Romantic status of a made object in relation to natural and supernatural orders of being.

This is certainly true of his "disordering" of Hass's "The Image," as it appears in *Notes for Echo Lake:*

> The child brought blue women from the creek
> Woman with a sunflower and woman with a stave
> (The match may never light)
>
> The child brought the world forward
> from the wall on a torn page
> They are dressing in red this season
>
> She tells him about horses
> The sun smiled during the night
> They are dressed in grey
>
> The child brought two women from the creek
> They counted their own number
> Each requires a name[52]

In "The Image," the child brings blue clay from the creek, which the woman then fashions into figures that correspond to living beings. In Palmer's text, the child brings blue women from the creek, as if the ritual of making were unnecessary, the child having direct access to the magical order of being. But it could also be said that the child is bringing the *words* "blue women" from the creek, since he also brings "the world forward / from the wall on a torn page." His understanding of the world develops gradually through his growing abilities to manipulate preexisting social and linguistic codes.[53] Parents and teachers guide the child: in Hass's poem, this is done nonverbally, through the sculpted figures, but in Palmer's poem, "She *tells* him about horses." But the book of world is never complete; its pages are torn, and there are always walls preventing complete understanding. Thus, the child cannot truly comprehend his magical encounter with the two women until they are numbered and *named.* They require a name, for words, not things, connect the natural and the supernatural orders, the real and the imaginary worlds.

The utopian longing for immediate experience found in Hass's poem, hearkening back to the more idyllic work of figures like Williams and Oppen, is countered by Palmer's more self-conscious but no less utopian awareness of the mediating force of language, inherited from precursors such as Duncan and Spicer. Even when Hass shares in this knowledge, his poems are suffused with a desire to return to the world before what Walter Benjamin calls "the Fall of language-mind."[54] Although, as in "Meditation at Lagunitas," "a word is elegy to what it signifies," we can still look for

> . . . moments when the body is as numinous
> as words, days that are the good flesh continuing.
> Such tenderness, those afternoons and evenings,
> saying *blackberry, blackberry, blackberry.*[55]

To which Palmer would reply:

> Letters of the world. Bright orange poppy next to white rose next to blue spike of larkspur and so on. Artichoke crowding garlic and sage. Hyssop, marjoram, orange mint, winter and summer savory, oregano, trailing rosemary, fuchsia, Dutch iris, day lily, lamb's tongue, lamb's ears, blackberry, feverfew, lemon verbena, sorrel, costmary, never reads it as it is, "poet living tomb of his / games."[56]

The world's plenitude blossoms around us, but we can never read it as it is for to read the world at all is know it only at a distance. A poetry written continually in such knowledge risks living in a tomb of verbal games, but opens us to the endless possibilities of utterance as well.

6

In the Fullness of Time

If there is a single tension in the utopian dynamic of contemporary poetry, it is that between immediacy and historicity, between the sufficiency of the indwelling moment and the desire for that sufficiency that ranges through the temporal continuum. In the four preceding chapters we have seen how a number of groups of experimental poets from the thirties through the eighties have attempted, through various historically conditioned strategies, to reconcile, or at least come to terms with, this basic tension. Having inherited both the problems and the resources of Romantic and Modernist traditions, poets like Ashbery or Duncan deploy modes of discourse in ways that embody the conditions of the present (keeping in mind that "the present" is always in flux) and still maintain some version of historical consciousness. True utopian thinking requires this sense of historicity to an extraordinary degree, but as I have argued, that sense is itself contingent on "the Messianic cessation of happening," the moment of fulfilled potential that exists within and beyond any creative—or revolutionary—act. Because, as Benjamin puts it, "every second of time [is] the strait gate through which the Messiah might enter," the immediate moment maintains a privileged position in any utopian endeavor, and this is nowhere more true than in contemporary poetry, most of which depends upon the immediacy of sense or thought for its stock-in-trade. No poem, however, can rest merely upon momentary plenitude; the poem enters the "time of the now" only because of its simultaneous awareness of its own historicity, or as Bloch puts it, the

utopian margins which surround actuality with *real and objective possibility*. Consequently every work which represents and informs this possibility (and every work would accord with the *per definitionem* of "significance") is full of augmented horizon problems; and its own level depends on the level of such problems. Therefore great works of art can dispense least of all with the creative touch of poetic anticipation—not the concealment or repression but the pre-semblance of what, objectively, is still latent in the world.[1]

The identification of that "pre-semblance" in a work of art is never a simple matter, and it is made especially difficult in any text that is concerned with the nature of time itself. How does one define the "horizon problems" of a text when it is about those very problems of definition, and indeed, is formally constituted by them? And yet for our purposes, these are some of the most crucial works, for the utopian propensity is most active, takes on the most palpable form, when engaged in argument with time, the repressive tyrant of the work as well as its potential liberator. In their recognition of temporal motion and the potentiality of historical events, such texts acknowledge the power of the *novum*, "the real possibility of the not-yet-known."[2] As Bloch says elsewhere, "Time *is* only because something happens, and where something happens, there time is."[3] Thus any work self-consciously concerned with time is an event in itself; it disturbs the placid surface of predictable daily affairs. In Benjamin's terms, time in the work of art is the messianic subject *ne plus ultra* (hence his involvement with Kafka and Proust), for by its very being it rejects the tepid assumptions of historicism, and like the historical materialist himself, "leaves it to others to be drained by the whore called 'Once upon a time' in historicism's bordello."[4] Instead, a work of such self-consciousness can "blast open the continuum of history," moving or arresting time in order to redefine our normative beliefs in historical continuity.

This is precisely the effect of those works of William Bronk which have to do with time, though it could be said that Bronk's entire opus is in some ways an extended meditation on the theme of self in time. Because we are bounded by our temporality and plagued with an inescapable awareness of mortality, the self-made worlds about which Bronk's poetry always moves shape themselves against the contours of time passing, while simultaneously struggling against this necessity.[5] Bronk explicitly contrasts time and space in this regard: the temporal experience emphasizes our estrangement from the world (hence the need to build our own worlds); the spatial experience somehow satisfies us. Bronk comes to this conclusion in "The World In Time and Space":

> If there is a shape to the world in terms of time
> and space—our own or, by concessions to shapes
> of others, received—if there is such a shape
> —in part there is—note that the words we use
> referring to time, as *temporary* for one
> or *temporal,* admit our diffidence
> toward any shape we give the world by time.
>
> The shapes of space share less of this distrust.
> We acknowledge chaotic recalcitrance
> in space, its endlessness both ways, the great,

and small, and yet respect the finite shape
of bounded places, as much as to say they are true.
Some absolute of shape is stated there
which satisfies the need that makes this shape.

How strange that after all it is rarely space
but time we cling to, unwilling to let it go.[6]

Typical of the honed abstractions of Bronk's statement-language, the last lines quietly throw the poem open to previously unstated doubts, undermining the hard-won assurances of the first two stanzas. Why, after such secure, eloquent gestures indicating otherwise, does he choose to assert that it is "time we cling to, unwilling to let it go"?

The answer, I think, is held within the key word "diffidence." If we want to fix our place in the world through the medium of time, rest secure in a given set of historical assumptions, understand reality from the vantage point of a single comprehensive moment, we also feel that we must reject such security, insisting on the radically *temporary* quality of any one conception of time. Time is anything but recalcitrant, as Bronk calls space; its essential subjectivity is such that we can always reconsider any "shape" we have imposed upon it. Yet we cannot relinquish the idea of time itself (which is always experienced as "the now"); it is the medium of possibility in which preconceived sequences of time, and the social conditions that fix such sequences, make them appear, as it were, eternal, are continually subverted or "blasted open." Thus, in "The Now Rejects Time and Eternity," we can understand why Bronk declares "I want to throw the idea of time away" and instead valorize "the now." Here is the complete text of that poem:

If I say not eternity either, it would be
for the reason, and only the reason, I suspect the word.
Unwisely perhaps; but it thinks of time.
Its meaning relies on time. I suspect it for that:
I want to throw the idea of time away,
or try to. To be without it. It's a little like
with no tools, to build nothing, and yet
to call it something, or more, to know it is
something. The tools of time. Without time's terms,
can we think at all? Yet time and eternity
are wrong, distract from now by the sequences
of time, or the eternal lack of consequence.
The now! Has there ever been, will there ever be,
not now? No, always. Only now![7]

Bronk's rhetoric here is particularly subtle. Again, we must note that time is related to "sequences" and that eternity is related to the "lack of consequence." Within this conception of temporality, *nothing ever happens*—all events are random and meaningless, and time itself becomes paltry and insignificant. In contrast to this, Bronk would like to dispense with time and "with no tools, to build nothing, and yet / to call it something, or more, to know it is / something." Here the idea of building, or of labor, is most telling, for in the time world he is presently forced to inhabit, labor is alienated labor, and for one of Bronk's impatience, therefore pointless. What Bronk wants to build—although by the very nature of his enterprise he cannot admit it—is significant time, meaningful events—in short, history. But history for Bronk is the most "utopian" construct of all; and historicity, as we shall soon see, is that one idea against which he deploys some of his most devastating rhetorical devices.

First, however, we must note that some of Bronk's poems express a strong desire for a structured, or at least a more teleological, experience of time. Rather than valorize the now in a critique of sequential, delimited time, such a poem as the frankly titled "We Want the Mark of Time" criticizes the repetitive endlessness of the continuum. In this way, too, possibility is again closed off, and the only alternative becomes the poem's apocalyptic closure:

> How shall we think of time without a change?
> The mark we do not cross was reached before.
> The present is very long and has been long.
>
> Oh, it is with desire we read of suns
> that some day burn themselves to darkness. At night
> we search the sky for such a sign: that there
> should be time, an ending. We want the mark of time.[8]

I take "the mark of time" to again signify meaningful time, even if meaning can only be found in "an ending." Time without a change is time without history: in his passion for totality, Bronk acknowledges historical difference only to deny it, as in his poem with the equally revealing title, "The Greeks, the Chinese, Or Say the Mayans." No single set of historical events, and indeed, not even history in its entirety is enough to convince him: for Bronk, like the poet of Ecclesiastes, nothing has ever changed.[9] In Bronk's work the force of desire is transhistorical. The human texture of history, the struggle of culture and its rewards, may provide solace, may even become sources of love, but can never finally satisfy us. As he says in "That Little Variance: Extensions On a Theme From Joseph Conrad,"

> It is too little to say that time is short. If it stretched
> wherever, no matter. It extends wherever. Add on,

add on. The units of time—hours, days,
dismay us by their extension. Time which divides
anywhere we divide it, goes on.

These long divisions mean nothing in human terms.
Divide or multiply, add on, subtract,
and any piece is all simply in not
being all, in incompleteness. Time which is gone
while still anticipated is incomplete.[10]

The context of the poem, the gentleman addressing other gentlemen, ironically underscores its theme: the speech circles its subject endlessly, and the poem itself stops with a dash.[11] Just as time is endless, incomplete and dissatisfying, so too is any human attempt to articulate that condition.

Bronk's view—or rather, views—of time, are thus typical of the pervasive ambiguity of his work. This is not to say that Bronk celebrates or even endorses ambiguity—at least not within individual texts, read in isolation. Each of his positions is usually asserted with the utmost conviction, despite the fact that another of his poems may subvert or even contradict that first position. But then, it is difficult to read a single Bronk poem in isolation: the structure of his individual volumes, and of *Life Supports,* the collected poems, invites the reader to consider the poetry as an ongoing act of writing, a continuous inscribing of consciousness upon the medium of time. Like Robert Duncan, whom he otherwise resembles very little, Bronk implicitly subscribes to the notion of the self as text as world. Bronk's poetry, his world, functions within time: it is written over time, and the reader is especially conscious of time moving within it as he goes from poem to poem. The epistemological shifts which occur within and between poems, their paradoxes and negations, are, in this regard, necessary products of time: the record of consciousness could emerge in no other form. As Bronk says in "The Poems: All Concessions Made,"

The poems (are they?) (such as they are), stay
with me or seem to. I turn away
sometimes, pretending alone, to do something else.
It is as though they wait—as if there.
I find them there. Their brief and still suspense
is the pause of performers, hearing applause on the stage.
The pause confirms them, of course, but they need me
to resume, are confident I mean to return.
Coming back, (I do) I find them there.
They are waiting for me. Well, we have to go on.
For no reason except that we started once.
That isn't a reason. It isn't reasonable.

> We concede so much. What don't we concede?
> I wish I had something; and the poems are there.[12]

No wonder then that Bronk displays such an ambiguous attitude toward time! Its continuity, and within that, its divisions, its stops and starts, arbitrary or natural as they come to appear, control his creative life; his identity as a poet depends upon his ability to write not only within but about time as well. The poems wait for him; his life and theirs are bound together, and time controls their fate. Each poem begins in the now and the poet goes on with his utterance from there: the poem is what remains with him after all concessions (and Bronk does not have to name them; we know all too well what they are) have been made. The poem, in the end, will redeem the poet's time.

But if this is really true, and Bronk's poems can really be read as gateways into a redemptive or messianic future, we must still account for the poet's determined critique of historicity, which is a crucial source for what would ordinarily be considered his "dark" or "existential" vision. This critique may be regarded on the one hand as ideological: the subtle arguments which dispel the appearance of historical change and cultural difference could be used to endorse and maintain a conservative defense of the status quo. On the other hand, Bronk's view of transhistorical desire is at least potentially revolutionary: it is explicitly anti-ideological in its overarching suspicion of stated human motives, and appears dedicated to the persistent subversion of reified patterns of thought and belief. This particular play of ideas (which, like all such intellectual tensions in Bronk's work, is essentially dialectical) is most clearly observed in the prose meditations that make up the volume *The New World*. These essays, occasioned by Bronk's trips to the Mayan and Incan ruins of Central and South America, are executed in a language as rhetorically elevated and rhythmically varied as the poems; and therefore may be considered not as an exposition of his poetic ideas, but as the prose complement to the lean, measured patterns of argument that mark the poems so distinctly. These texts are by no means "philosophical" in the traditional sense of the term, and could even be taken as a poetic deconstruction of the particular generic assumptions of the philosophical essay. Their appearance as simple travel pieces in itself assails conventional reader expectations. Indeed, the concrete historical details of the travelogue and the authoritative, albeit speculative universals of the philosophical essay may be viewed as antitheses that Bronk has not so much reconciled in *The New World* as set definitively against each other.[13] The fate of a "primitive," "alien" culture, which at first seems, in its historical and geographic specificity, to be radically *other*, is made to appear no more or less meaningful or consequential than our own: the revenge of the universal against the particular. And yet the grand philosophical vistas that absorb vast differences in time and place eventually smack against the engineered stone of otherness represented by the ruins of Machu Picchu and Copan: the revenge of the particular against the universal. In either case, we are stripped of our intellectual pretensions; we can neither rejoice in the advanced state of our civilization nor share in the comparable achievements of previous ones.

Bronk's critique of history thus takes place in the ruins of time themselves, abandoned battlefields where a sophisticated but appreciably different human culture struggled to make sense of the very issues that Bronk himself wishes to raise. In "At Tikal," we are told of the Mayas' elaborate calendar, their worshipful accumulation and recording of time in divisions so complex and painstaking "as to suggest that time itself was the object of that worship."[14] As Bronk recreates these ancient calculations, he gradually realizes that

> It is the absurdity of time that although it is a finite measurement, it has neither in logic nor experience any beginning or end. It is true that experience would seem to indicate beginnings and endings for individuals. Time then is like a thread or cord laid up by the twisting together of many individual fibers of varying lengths and definite measure. The individual fibers end, and the cord stretches on indefinitely. There is an idea of time as pure continuance, existing endlessly before now and after now—a finally absurd idea if time is a measure, for a pure, abstract continuance is immeasurable. Any segment is all.[15]

It is at this point of realization in the essay that fact suddenly gives way to speculation. And yet despite this realization, Bronk notes that humans usually regard time as "a measure of some new condition, of some change"—in other words, time as history, for the new condition, whether mythical or actual, indicates the importance of events breaking into the infinite sameness of the continuum. Thus "it is evident that one speaks of time as two things—as an indefinite continuance and as a finite duration of a special condition."[16] These views of time are, of course, those we have seen at work in the poetry. But in the essay, they abut each other in the following remarkable configuration:

> The very unit of time is a unit of change, of the alternations of light and dark, and the special and temporary concomitants which, by association, seem to accompany the coming of darkness or a new day. Thus, brief durations have the greatest validity and although a long duration is not impossible, its content is so altered by change as it lengthens as to be lost or to become meaningless. It is as though we were counting oranges and found that for some time now we had actually been counting the seeds of oranges, or orange trees, or perhaps even apples, and were not able to say at what point the change

had happened. We have been counting, not a finite duration, but an indefinite continuance which is uncountable, and have been using a unit of change to count the unchanging.[17]

Here Bronk seeks to correct, or at least set in what he deems to be a more proper perspective, our conventional view of eventful (changing, historical) time. Against the unchanging we set what is essentially a fiction of change, and like all fictions, all self-made worlds, this one can more or less suffice—until tested against the skeptical consciousness inspired by the simultaneous strangeness and familiarity of Tikal. As the essay concludes,

> The expressions of time are arbitrary and variable and even absurd, assuming as they do a beginning and an end for which there is no basis in experience. We experience changes whose duration we note and measure as though they were all—or even anything. But we experience as well a continuing present which neither we nor the Mayas approach or depart from, a present which neither develops nor declines. It is there. The changes do not express it.[18]

So time as measure and change is an illusion, but an illusion with which we will apparently never dispense. What happens when we do momentarily dispense with that illusion is the subject of "Copan: Historicity Gone." Like "At Tikal," the essay moves from fact—in this case, the detail of the stonework of Copan, the Mayan city that was apparently abandoned by its inhabitants—to bold speculation. And like "At Tikal," the ongoing movement of its argumentation is such that the essay resists being excerpted, depending on the cumulative effect of its rhetoric to bring the reader to its drastically unorthodox position. That position, stated directly near the end of the essay, is that "Whatever we are, we are not historical." Because the Mayas gave up counting time in Copan and left the city, "we feel at home there because, however remote or alien its terminology, we sense through all our ignorance that time and history have been here once." The coupling of anteriority with immediacy here is startling. Historical time is ordinarily taken to assert itself through its *presence* when we visit such a site as Copan,; but for Bronk, it is asserted through its *absence*. Indeed, the metaphysical experience adumbrated here is not the reinforcement of historical time, of change, of loss or of progress, but their complete dissolution beneath the unyielding pressure of what Bronk, throughout his work, has only been able to call unsatisfied desire. Desire is that which strips away the mask of historical difference, the stone mask of the planet Venus in the East Court of Copan, the fleshly mask we face in our own modern bedroom mirrors. And as Bronk says,

One of the strongest impressions that we have is that under the mask and metaphor something is there though it is not perhaps man that is there. There is something which is. Nothing else matters. Copan is a liberation. It is all gone, emptied away. To see it is to see ourselves gone, to see us freed from the weight of our own world and its limitations.[19]

Through such a passage as this, we may come to recognize the utopian substrate of Bronk's work. To be sure, the dissolution of history is an operation performed by some more readily than others—we need only think of the Mayas after the arrival of the Spanish to realize that historicity simply does not depart through the exercise of mere consciousness. And yet Bronk is right: Copan, or at least his vision of Copan, is a liberation, and it is to his great credit that he tells us just what we are liberated from:

We are happy at Copan to witness our own destruction and how we survive it. If something may be said to happen, what happens to us is not what happens. The evident destruction of Copan is witness to this as we, in our lives, are witness to the same things. We are delivered from our continuous failures and frustrations. Perhaps more importantly, we are delivered from our self-limited successes, the awful banalities of the good life.[20]

The awful banalities of the good life: with a single gesture, Bronk exposes the danger of historicity, the rarely noticed ideological link between a self-satisfied "knowledge" of history and the grossly complacent view of the present as the best of times. Bronk's "historicity" is much like Benjamin's "historicism," which drives him to declare, in that famous sentence, that "There is no document of civilization which is not at the same time a document of barbarism."[21] The difference lies, of course, in the issue of human action: for Benjamin, as a Marxist, the alternative to "universal history" is revolution. For Bronk, "The good society and the good life are more than we can imagine. To devise them or to assert and defend their devising is not the point." Yet this too is a protest against "empty time," time which, as we are limited in perceiving it, moves against the dramatic imposition of historical events, until all such events appear equally absurd.

But it is not only time which can render our conventional view of history absurd, if not worse; it is the nature of life within time as well. In the final essay of *The New World,* "Copan: Unwillingness, the Unwilled," Bronk addresses the idea of "life" or "being" so as to shed more light on the problem of human motivation and effort. This essay is unique among the six pieces that comprise the volume in that there are no explicit references whatsoever to the physical site or history of the ruin. Only the very last sentence alludes to Copan at all, when Bronk states that "our responses are presences that tower around us, seemingly solid as stone." Through this rhetorical strategy, historical difference is again dismissed: universal states of consciousness such as Bronk ventures to posit obviate what we would judge to be crucial distinctions of time and space, culture, class, and gender. In their place we find the poet's most thoroughgoing metaphysical discourse, which is determined to root out any hypostatizations of life that do not hold life itself as the absolute.

What Bronk means by "life" (and depending on his argument, he will also use such words as "being" "desire" or simply "it") is that force that moves through the world, especially through human action, as a primary motivation or intentionality. We are a part of this: Bronk is particularly hard on all forms of dualistic thinking. However, it is basic to the human condition that we attempt to differentiate our desires from life's desire, which by its very nature is entirely apart from us and unknowable. Probably echoing Melville in *The Confidence Man* (about which he writes in *The Brother in Elysium*), Bronk declares:

> The human situation seems less a come-as-you-are party than a party to which we are bidden to come as our favorite character and, though we are sometimes cheap or shy, we do fairly well. We put on the costume and badges, the mental attitudes, the facial and vocal expressions of *something,* of *someone.* Such an action gives shape and clarity to our desires, gives them poles and simplicity; it sets us up as some marked-off existent. It is of course evasive.[22]

Such a statement places Bronk in the company of the many distanced observers of the vanity of human wishes, but the integrity of his complex thought, especially as expressed in the formal contours of his prose, makes him far more than a mere skeptic. For when he instructs us in his beliefs, the result is yet another extraordinarily fruitful set of ambiguities:

> If we are not to falsify life, but to have it for what it is, we must leave ourselves open to it and undefended, observant of what may happen, since our private will is not relevant and we are not capable of apprehending or assisting any other will, and what we observe and feel is perhaps less will than being and the nature of being. We have made up complicated frameworks of activity and attitude on the foundation that somehow we grasp what may be wanted from us, some challenge or imperative. The challenges and imperatives may not be anything like each other in any respect except in this: that they assume our receiving them. But in experience (and on the contrary) nothing is revealed to us of what our nature may be, or of what we must do.[23]

As is often the case with Bronk's statements of this sort, either a "right" or "left" (or perhaps a "passive" or an "active") interpretation is possible.[24] On the conservative side, because we cannot know life's intentionality, because life is apart from us and our desires may not be at all consonant with it despite our "complicated frameworks," we may as well adopt a passive attitude in the face of life, accepting our existence as the "instrument" of a remote other. On the progressive side, Bronk's existential endorsement of an open, undefended stance in life allows for the entrance of an apocalyptic (which is to say, historically unmediated) but still entirely viable mode of being. Because nothing is revealed to us of what our nature may be, we can never simply accept our life as a given, but instead act in accordance with our perception of life's desire, as ultimately futile an act as that might be. Furthermore, since "there are things we feel, certain angers, rejoicings, fears" which "come from beyond our skin like approaches to us, like messages," we can be moved to act in ways that utterly transcend mere self-interest. Thus, Bronk's view of human motivation and action is both exhilarating and terrifying: like Spicer responding to the outside (and Bronk in his essay on Machu Picchu actually speaks of the Mayas worshipping an "Outside God"), he sees our creativity as a response to a force beyond our control and comprehension, but more genuinely a part of us than any aspect of our life that we ordinarily deem to be our own.

We emerge from the essays of *The New World* with a fuller understanding of Bronk's historical agon, as reason turns upon the notion of human rationality and the creative faculties unmask themselves to expose the emptiness of human creativity. The concept of progress likewise falls victim to Bronk's rhetoric, for when human motivation is lost to history, and history itself has ceased to be the repository of human achievement, then progress, which promises higher forms of civilization opening in futurity, becomes nothing more than another fiction. The utopian propensity should wither in such climates of thought; but Bronk, we must recall, is more than a mere thinker—he is a poet, for whom the sensuous form of the poem encompasses his highly mediated relation to the ideas he expresses. Consider, then, the poem from which comes the epigraph to chapter 1, "About Dynamism, Desire and Various Fictions":

> Also the Golden Age was a dark time
> if there was one. I think it is now and was not
> ever. It is dark now as it always was.
>
> The thing I wanted to tell you is how we propose
> a drama, sort of, a story of our lives
> which requires changes—sequences of time,

such that once there was this or something else
—dark, say, or the Golden Age, and then
something happened and *this* came about.

Well I don't think it did. What I want
you to know is that nothing happened and nothing can,
that stories are fictions, truth doesn't tell one,

that the beautiful is that, nothing more,
and enough, no story, nothing to do or tell.[25]

In his essay on Bronk, Henry Weinfield observes of this poem that

The Golden Age is refuted, not obviously *per se*, but in order paradox-
ically to recapitulate its essential human content: the image of social
relations as pure harmony, and the dialectic of loss and yearning which
elicits this image.[26]

We may take this as the starting point for our discussion, noting that
Weinfield too sees Bronk's rhetoric as standing in an antithetical rela-
tionship to this theme. Certainly, this poem includes a number of those
themes we have previously remarked: the critique of historical change,
the refutation of sequential time, the fictionality of any human ordering
of reality, and the insistence upon "truth" and "the beautiful" as forces
outside and unaffected by those fictions. But here, these ideas are
brought to bear directly on the myth of the Golden Age, that most
enduring image of utopian fulfillment. Traditionally, the Golden Age is
always posited in the remote past; likewise the "dark times" of various
periods of history are regarded as having been and gone: promise and
threat distanced from the present so as to allow for the perpetuation of
the status quo, as well as for the struggle against it. Bronk, in keeping
with his belief in "the now," undercuts tradition to the extent that the
present becomes both the best and worst of times, without the possibility
of substantive change. Furthermore, by conflating the best and worst,
now as in the past, the poem seems to eliminate all possibility of change;
time is ongoing and undifferentiated, as is the poem's argument, appar-
ently beginning in the middle with the word "Also." And because
"nothing happened and nothing can," the future, bearing the possibility
of action, is rigorously excluded from the poem's discourse.

We must remind ourselves, however, that the poem itself is an act; it
"happens," though it seeks rhetorically to deny itself in such terms. The
poem is a story, a telling, and meant to be taken as truth; and in this
respect it is caught within a paradox, for what it *is* contradicts what it *says*.
We cannot doubt the completely earnest form of its utterance; its won-
derfully measured, highly compressed syntax (note the finely ordered

sequence of ideas it offers from moment to moment, line to line) and its final evocation of truth and beauty convince us of its integrity and high seriousness. Thus we are led to conclude that the poem's formal and rhetorical strategies are meant to raise questions, to propose the terms of the debate, although the poet himself cannot offer an affirmative response. What we are left with is the sense of continuance. Truth and beauty as metaphysical sources of value remain relevant terms in an ongoing dialogue; tradition in its poetic, philosophical and historical contexts survives within the text, and indeed, takes on new life, because of the text's authoritative denials.

These denials are at times so direct in their articulation that they are able to overturn all that precedes them within the poem. In such a piece as "The Story of Mankind From Earliest Times to the Present Day," the final couplet echoes throughout the rest of the text, forcing the reader to reconsider the more readily acceptable argument it develops:

> We are so set on making stories, asleep
> even, only the mind moving, lying intent
> to stroke whatever comes to it, awake
> while the body sleeps, identifying sounds
> with events, feelings with faces, picking out
> from the day's debris whatever will make do.
>
> Awake, our invention finds room to move,
> sets up itself in three dimension as if
> it were there, assigns us almost consistent roles
> to hold from day to day, necessitates
> a past we must have had, and a time to come
> where, even now, the story begins to be true.
>
> What may, in fact, go on, if indeed it does,
> has nothing at all to take from the story we tell.[27]

A poem like this can make us a little giddy, given the intellectual range it demands for itself through its title and the discourse which follows after it. What at first appears to be a story offering universal principles with claims upon the entirety of human events, proves to be the story of all such stories, which in turn denies the validity of any stories we might tell. For Bronk, to be human is to invent fictions—dreams, personal lives, systems of politics, philosophy, religion, and history itself—all of which validate our assumptions concerning time, change, and consequence. But for all of that, the stories we tell, the fictions we invent, are unconnected to "What may, in fact, go on, if indeed it does." It is quite beside the point to argue against such an assertion: in the very rhetorical structure of the poem, which allows for such an assertion to be made, we find the poem's controlling thematic tension, the source of its linguistic dynamic. The poem bears witness to the underlying passion of historical self-consciousness, for even as Bronk denies history, he must inevitably couch his language in historical terms. The matter of the poem, as a history, "necessitates / a past we must have had, and a time to come / where, even now, the story begins to be true." It is not that Bronk is victimized by his metaphors or that, in the end, he even seeks to escape them. Rather, by virtue of the fact that he is a poet, he is inescapably wed to the historical process of linguistic production. As he says in "His Poems":

> Alone sometimes, I remember how certain things
> were said: that's what we were talking about
> and the statement was made that—and then, oh . . . yes![28]

Such a warm affirmation as this is difficult to find in Bronk's poetry, in which, as should be obvious by now, desire moves with such bounding energy that most poems appear to question the very idea of resolution, regardless to what extent they seem to close or come to rest. In work so riddled with contraries as this, the dominant form of belief is doubt, and knowledge is an admission of ignorance. Contentment and pleasure are seductions, and while Bronk will bow to Eros, as he will bow to other gods, it is always because he knows that in the end he can cast them off. The erotic perfection of the material world, to which one can only respond with affirmation, receives the poet's praise because, just as he affirms the metaphors of his poems, he considers the world itself to be a metaphor too:

> Such pleasure as I have felt in good times
> in landscapes, urges that memory discard all
> but the scene itself, forgetting pleasure, as if
> the scene were an absolute (regardless of me,
> what I saw and felt) the scene's particulars
> a gauge of value: let the world be that
> or more that, made-so, as we might make
> if we could, and the scene had value of its own.
>
> We see these Edens in the world, believe in them.
> Was the first garden such as Adam could leave,
> Eve leave, and be really elsewhere, apart
> from the presence whose metaphor the garden was,
> feeling the absence? Landscape is metaphor
> and only metaphor. But, oh, I have loved it so.[29]

This poem is called "Paradise Now and Then," and it is one of the few poems in Bronk's opus in which the utopian propensity is expressed less in terms of absence and counterpoint than in terms of presence and resolution. Paradise is perfect sufficiency; so it was for Adam and Eve as they left the Garden, and so it is for Bronk, who can experience and believe in that sufficiency, at least momentarily, despite the knowledge that Paradise is a metaphor in which the primary term has been withdrawn, or rather, has absconded with Itself. In Bronk's ceaseless quest for a source of value, landscapes in good times (points in space, moments in time) can suddenly become an absolute, a gauge of value; and despite the ubiquitous insistence on metaphor, we suddenly sense the immanent presence of utopian possibility. This is the fullness of time, a true instance of the *Jetztzeit.* Despite the knowledge of original loss that forces the poet to use the conditional and acknowledge the metaphoric quality of his discourse, he cannot deny his pleasure, the libidinal force of which seems to enfold the continuum of history in its warm embrace, resolving the human struggle back into natural plenitude. Bronk looks back at Paradise: his gesture is the converse of Adam's in *Paradise Lost,* when, in Books XI and XII, he stands with Michael and looks forward from Paradise. In the former case, history is cancelled; in the latter, history unfolds. The collective human action that Adam sees projected before him, "The Story of Mankind," is for Bronk, as we have seen, an elaborate fiction, "as we might make / if we could." Yet beyond Bronk's contradictions—through musical form, we might say, rather than argumentation—it is clear how resolutely he places himself within this tradition of poetic discourse. The paradisiacal moment, the utopian possibility, the messianic entrance into the future: even *if* they are metaphors, they are what elicit the poet's declaration of love.

For in "Paradise Now and Then," as in "The Story of Mankind" and "About Dynamism, Desire and Various Fictions," the key term is "if" or "as if." One could almost say that all of Bronk's poetry is written in the conditional, and the conditional is always related to the future. "As if" is just a step away from "not yet," Bloch's imaginative operator that transforms the present, maintaining the potential for perfection under certain conditions at some future point in time.[30] And as if one could express such a state in a metaphor, Bronk writes "To Praise the Music," one of his most beautiful poems:

> Evening. The trees in late winter bare
> against the sky. Still light, the sky.
> Trees dark against it. A few leaves
> on the trees. Tension in their rigid branches as if
> —oh, it is all as if, but as if, yes,
> as if they sang songs, as if they praised.
> Oh, I envy them. I know the songs.

As if I know some other things besides.
As if; but I don't know, not more
than to say the trees know. The trees don't know
and neither do I. What is it keeps me from praise?
I praise. If only to say their songs,
say yes to them, to praise the songs they sing.
Envied music. I sing to praise their song.[31]

Conclusion: On Tradition

n John Ashbery's *A Wave* (1984), we find the following poem:

Purists Will Object

We have the looks you want:
The gonzo (musculature seemingly wired to the stars);
Colors like lead, khaki and pomegranate; things you
Put in your hair, with the whole panoply of the past:
Landscape embroidery, complete sets of this and that.
It's bankruptcy, the human haul,
The shining, bulging nets lifted out of the sea, and always a few
    refugees
Dropping back into the no-longer-mirthful kingdom
On the day someone sells an old house
And someone else begins to add on to his: all
In the interests of this pornographic masterpiece,
Variegated, polluted skyscraper to which all gazes are drawn,
Pleasure we cannot and will not escape.

It seems we were going home.
The smell of blossoming privet blanketed the narrow avenue.
The traffic lights were green and aqueous.
So this is the subterranean life.
If it can't be conjugated onto us, what good is it?
What need for purists when the demotic is built to last,
To outlast us, and no dialect hears us?[1]

This poem seems to anticipate and respond to my entire project, which
actually makes perfect sense, if, as Paul de Man tells us, "Poetry is the
foreknowledge of criticism."[2] The heterogeneity (I am tempted to say
"promiscuity") of Ashbery's work, "this pornographic masterpiece," the
high-spirited carnage he produces in the ruins of the utopian sublime,
forces the critic who wishes to read such poetry in the antithetical
manner I have proposed to instead accede and complete that "varie-
gated, polluted skyscraper to which all gazes are drawn." "No one listens

to poetry," says Jack Spicer at his glummest—but if they do, it's Ashbery
to whom they listen, since he has the looks they want. Ashbery is both
hedgehog and fox; he knows only one thing, what he calls in this poem
"the demotic"; but to know the demotic is actually to know as many
things as are necessary to survive in our ongoing, empty present. Thus
he is our most fashionable poet; he presents the surface of our ever-
changing, ever-the-same mass culture, just as George Oppen in *Of Being
Numerous* presents its underlying contradictions. When Ashbery appro-
priates a term like "gonzo" and all that it implies, he argues that fashion
has finally replaced high culture, and the purists who seek to recover or
even analyze tradition are simply no longer needed.

But one such purist, George Lukács, still describes the situation pre-
cisely:

> The dominance of fashion means that the form and quality of the
> product placed on the market is altered in short periods of time
> independently of the beauty or purpose of such alterations. *It is of the
> essence of the market that new things must be produced within definite periods of
> time,* things which must differ radically from that which preceded, and
> which cannot build upon the previous collected experience of produc-
> tion.[3]

Now it would be irresponsible of me to suggest that we may account for
the drastic shifts in style in American poetry of the last few decades by
considering them to be manifestations of the literary market economy,
transforming themselves in response to the capitalist demand for nov-
elty in production. Aside from the inherent "vulgarity" of such a sugges-
tion, we may note that these various styles do indeed build, at least to
some extent, "upon the previously collected experience of production."
For the speaker of "Purists Will Object," however, such insights might be
interesting, might even be true, but they are only one small part, rather
than an authoritative interpretation, of the contemporary scene. They
do nothing to remedy the inescapable "bankruptcy" of what, in the end,
we must call the humanist tradition, which, from the tone of the poem,
we are better off for having jettisoned.[4]

It may be that this book is merely a footnote to the great wager of
humanism being made in our time, or even a footnote to a footnote, if
one agrees with some of the views of contemporary poetry cited in the
first chapter. I hope I have answered such criticisms, for I believe that
poetry can still speak, however problematic its utterance, to our contem-
porary situation—what Marshall Berman calls "a modern age that has
lost touch with the roots of its own modernity."[5] If "the panoply of the
past," which for poets means a literary tradition, is to be viewed as
something more than "bulging nets lifted out of the sea," then what

might be termed a utopian refunctioning of our view of tradition is crucial, despite the fact that, as Berman points out in his history of modernism, the contradictions embedded in any concept of tradition lead us to doubt the validity of the concept entirely, especially when we are confronted by the constant flux of the present, where "all that is solid melts into air."

Highly self-conscious discussions of literary tradition, although they have never been entirely absent from the realm of criticism, are a distinct and pervasive feature of criticism in our century. Closely bound up with recent interrogations of canon, attempts to define the relation between tradition and the individual talent (which have at least their formal beginning, obviously, with T. S. Eliot) may be traced in part to the equally self-conscious sense of modernity—difference from the past— that Berman thoroughly documents. However, Paul de Man, in what amounts to a critique of such historicizing narratives of literary tradition, argues that "the ambivalence of writing is such that it can be considered both an act and an interpretative process that follows after an act with which it cannot coincide."[6] Thus, because the writer "is both the historian and the agent of his own language," it would seem that critical discourses which privilege historicized explanations of the text, from Eliot's ideal order of monuments to Harold Bloom's Oedipal agon, are to be held in suspicion. The problematic modernity that calls forth the notion of tradition is not so much a matter of historical periodicity but an intrinsic feature of writing as an act. De Man, partaking in the post-Nietzschean "joyful wisdom" of deconstruction, posits a utopian function in language itself, especially literary language, because of the "persistent temptation of literature to fulfill itself in a single moment."[7] As he explains:

> Moments of genuine humanity thus are moments at which all anteriority vanishes, annihilated by the power of an absolute forgetting. Although such a radical rejection of history may be illusory or unfair to the achievements of the past, it nevertheless remains justified as necessary to the fulfillment of our human destiny and as the condition for action.[8]

De Man, as is his wont, both admonishes and liberates. The stress he places on the temporal ambivalence of writing cannot altogether forbid speculation on the inner workings of literary history; rather, we must become aware—like some of the poets we have discussed—of how, given the proper historical conditions, the historical dimension of the text can dissolve into "the now." That the now, as we have seen, can constitute the fullness or the emptiness of time, depending upon the historical narrative read off from the text, in a sense rescues the study of tradition from the deconstructive abyss into which, however, it must always peer.

Equally important (and equally troubling) to a utopian refunctioning of modern studies of tradition is the tendency observed by Michael André Bernstein. In comparing various theories, such as Eliot's or Bloom's, Bernstein notes that

> even the most antithetical of these polemics participate in a surprising consensus about the nature and function of their subject. The exemplary masters of "the tradition" may be entirely different in each formulation, and the consequences of the successor's indebtedness to the canon may be mapped according to radically contrasting assumptions, but the prior existence of that canon as a coherent hierarchy is itself never put into doubt.[9]

Significantly, this insight arises out of a study of Robert Duncan; and Bernstein goes on to argue that Duncan's seminal notion of the *grand collage* "enacts the different paths a searcher for knowledge may follow, and so, just as there is no one master tradition, so there is no single collage that stands in a privileged relationship to the other possible efforts."[10] Tradition, then, is always, at least to some extent, a synthetic matter; the major poet is capable of assimilating, even inventing his or her precursors. In the twentieth century, the "tradition" of Stevens or the "tradition" of Pound are thus critical fictions, to which active poets rarely subordinate themselves. As Terry Eagleton observes:

> What is transmitted by tradition is not 'things', and least of all 'monuments', but 'situations'—not solitary artefacts but the strategies that construct and mobilize them. It is not that we constantly revaluate a tradition; tradition *is* the practice of ceaselessly excavating, safeguarding, violating, discarding and reinscribing the past. There is no tradition other than this, no set of ideal landmarks that then suffer modification.[11]

Eagleton argues that this revolutionary view of tradition can only emerge as concomitant to a Marxist understanding of history; thus "tradition is nothing other than a series of spasms or crises within class history, not the scattered letters of an invisible word."[12] It is worth noting, however, that this revolutionary view of tradition, set against the systematizing of Eliot or Bloom, is in itself profoundly traditional. Without discounting Eagleton's Marxist interpretation, we can trace its origins back through the theologically inclined Walter Benjamin to his friend Gershom Scholem. Eagleton concedes as much in his book on Benjamin (why else would he be attracted to the Kabbalistic metaphor of "scattered letters"?), but here is the crucial passage from Scholem's "Revolution and Tradition as Religious Categories in Judaism" which makes the correspondence fully legible:

> Tradition undergoes changes with the times, new facets of its meaning shining forth and lighting its way. Tradition, according to its mystical sense, is Oral Torah [that is, historically contingent interpretation], precisely because every stabilization of the text would hinder and destroy the infinitely moving, the constantly progressing and unfolding element within it, which would otherwise become petrified.[13]

It is difficult to avoid seeing the utopian quality of these utterances; indeed, from the contemporary standpoint, the idea of literary tradition and the study of its dynamics become in themselves signs of immanent utopian content. If the essence of the writer's relation to tradition is to be found in "reinscribing the past" so as to insure "the constantly progressing and unfolding element within it," then the writer must be Janus-faced, and the act of writing both reevaluates past tradition and projects it forward, toward a utopian horizon at which it will never arrive.

This brings us full circle to the first epigraph of this study and the poem by William Bronk from which it comes. The opening stanzas of "Some Musicians Play Chamber Music For Us" adumbrate the process that I have been describing. The continuum of tradition arises and perpetuates itself because, in the presence of a work of art, the new artist feels the necessity to produce "some response, a further phrase, its tone / asking perhaps, or adding, or simply 'yes.'" The result is

> a moving space
> constantly pushing outward, here, then there,
> then there, which becomes at all because it moves,
> because it holds itself to certain lines.[14]

The existence of the new work, and consequently that of the tradition, is dependent upon movement, but this "moving space" that is created by the response also "holds itself to certain lines." The line between past and future is never broken, but is rather sustained by the present response. That a poet in our time can so bravely articulate this knowledge provides a measure of hope that poetry will continue to "recollect forward" in a world that looks neither behind nor before, but obsessively at itself.

Appendix: Ernst Bloch and the Utopian Refunctioning of Marxism

Ernst Bloch is a figure for whom the fashionable term "problematic" is both perfectly appropriate and hopelessly insufficient: it can represent but in no way do justice to the entangled debates which inevitably emerge upon even the slightest consideration of Bloch's accomplishment. Ranging between the remote poles of vulgar materialism and flagrant mysticism, constantly dogged by the same Stalinism that preys upon his erstwhile friend Georg Lukács, Bloch is the "Western Marxist" *par excellence*. What is Marxism's relationship to its intellectual precursors, especially philosophical idealism, abstract utopian thought, and apocalyptic messianism? Can Marxism as a discursive practice really produce a totalized worldview that is still free of totalitarianism? To what extent do the arts escape the function of ideology as Marxism understands it, to win for themselves instead a "utopian function"? What is the task of the committed or revolutionary critic in examining cultural productions of the past and present? In the course of his work, Bloch provides, more or less, his own answers to all of these questions, but in such ways as to rarely satisfy even his most sympathetic readers. Then again, satisfaction is a dubious response to theoretical analysis, for satisfaction rarely opens us to the "not yet," that most pervasive operator in Bloch's infuriatingly original lexicon. Better to respond with "upright gait" *(aufrechter Gang)* and assert one's own position—or paradoxically, begin to daydream about the problem at hand and create, as in the title of one of Bloch's essays, "better castles in the sky."

Some of the most important and difficult passages in Bloch's criticism are concerned with the derivation and explanation of what he calls a cultural or ideological surplus *(uberschuss,* literally "overshot"). The term inevitably calls to mind Marx's notion of surplus value, extracted through the process of labor and eventually expropriated from the laborer by the capitalist. Artistic production, as a form of labor, can be partially understood in terms of a classical Marxist analysis of the eco-

nomic base, but because art also maintains its existence in the superstruc-
ture, its enduring value beyond that of mere ideology (or false
consciousness) has long posed a problem for Marxist aesthetics—and no
Marxist critic is more keenly aware of this than Bloch. Thus he describes
the inadequacy of the base/superstructure model quite plainly:

> It is relatively easy to grasp the equation economy = state, to be sure,
> not according to the way the beneficiaries of the time understood it,
> but according to Marxist terms. However, with regard to the fields of
> *art, religion,* and *philosophy,* the components predicated on the same
> illusory givens cannot be explained directly by the Marxist analysis or
> even partly by the base.[1]

And while Bloch certainly understands that "the superstructure is not
merely placed on the base externally like the masthead is attached to the
ship and passively conforms to all of its movements,"[2] it could be argued
that the dialectical twists and turns in his account of the utopian function
("a transcending one without transcendence"[3]) ultimately refine the
original materialist theory out of existence. For Bloch is haunted by his
heritage of German Romantic idealism, a heritage he frequently but
unsuccessfully tries to repress. As he suddenly blurts out in his remark-
able "A Philosophical View of the Novel of the Artist," "at the very least,
art must be against historicism, sociologism, and schematicism (for here
there is a tendency to obfuscate the subject of art itself) and must recall
the truth of a basic source."[4] Bloch's aesthetic theory is an extended
attempt to uncover art's "truth of a basic source" by just those dialectical
means that opponents of Marxism see as historicism, sociologism, and
schematicism. At the same time, the more rigorous historicists and
sociologists of Marxist aesthetic theory are bound to be dismayed, for
Bloch's elaborate speculations on the relations of art and ideology, while
appearing to be systematic and materialistic, are anything but. This,
however, is probably to Bloch's credit. Despite the frequent opacity of his
churning discourse, partly the result, no doubt, of his desire to remain
faithful to a restrictively narrow set of Marxist concepts (and this despite
his obviously unorthodox approach!), some startling insights emerge.

Crucial to Bloch's understanding of ideology, and hence of the base/
superstructure model in its entirety, is his distinction between ideology
and the "anticipatory illumination" *(Vor-Schein)* of utopia; or within ide-
ology itself, that which is mere false consciousness and that which may
come to be understood as a utopian surplus. As Bloch rightly observes:

> False consciousness alone would not be capable of producing one of
> the most important characteristics of ideology, i.e., the premature
> harmonizing of the social contradictions. Ideology is less comprehen-
> sible as the medium of a continuous cultural substratum without an

encounter with the utopian function. All this obviously exceeds the capacity of false consciousness that cannot invigorate or apologize for the specific social basis. Therefore, without the utopian function, the class ideologies would have only managed to achieve an ephemeral delusion and not the models of art, science, and philosophy. And it is precisely this surplus that forms and maintains the substratum of the cultural heritage, the morning that is present not only in the early period but more so during the full day of a society, even partly in the twilight of its decline.[5]

Because cultural production continues, due to a great extent to the accomplishments of the past, Bloch attempts to discern the substratum of culture at any point in history, which, as a surplus, will maintain its power to illuminate or inspire the labor of future generations and later societies. In his discussions of cultural heritage, Bloch does not dispense with the concept of ideology completely, because he understands how thoroughly the deceptive or repressive beliefs of a class system intermingle with the anticipatory or the utopian. Instead, he theorizes at some length, positing the utopian function within the ideologies of the "revolutionary rise . . . the sanctimonious flourishing, and finally the stage of spotted decline" and seeking works that best illustrate such relations.[6] Furthermore, the "anticipatory countermove" against the ideological status quo may be found exerting pressure against its most embellished features. Bloch summarizes: "When they refer mostly to *concentration,* they are known as *archetypes;* when they refer mostly to *perfection,* they are known as *ideals;* when they refer mostly to *meaning,* they are known as *allegories* and *symbols.*"[7] And like the three ideological moments of social history, these three structural categories in the ideology of a single point in time are subject to the utopian function as well.

What emerges then is a search for anticipatory illumination that is both diachronic and synchronic in its orientation, and certainly hair-raising in its potential for totalization. Yet for Bloch, this is as it should be: the *novum* is ubiquitous, identifiable in even the most regressive archetype or period of social degeneration; Frederic Jameson says of Bloch's work, "hope is *always* thwarted, the future is always something *other* than what we sought to find there, something ontologically excessive and necessarily unexpected."[8] What is expected always arrives but never as that which is expected. As Bloch notes, defining not only cultural heritage but by implication the task of the cultural critic, "in the final analysis, cultural heritage means the knowledge of what is missing that propels one to culture; separation of utopia from ideology in cultural works; keeping the promise of culture, which means building its house."[9]

If this suspiciously metaphysical discourse makes Bloch sound less like a Marxist than like a Hegelian version of Northrop Frye, it will be worthwhile to briefly compare his theory of art and ideology to that of a

critic who, although even more wide-ranging in his theoretical sympa-
thies, is taken today to be a major exponent of a Marxist view of
literature—Terry Eagleton. In *Criticism and Ideology*, which remains Ea-
gleton's most comprehensive examination of the subject, we are told,
amidst endless permutations of "general ideology," "authorial ideology,"
"aesthetic ideology," etc., that "there is no 'immanent' value—no value
which is not *transitive*. Literary value is a phenomenon which is *produced*
in that ideological appropriation of the text, that 'consumptional produc-
tion' of the work, which is the act of reading. It is always *relational* value:
'exchange-value.'"[10] This passage, which I take to be fairly representa-
tive of Eagleton's stance in his more recent works as well, indicates the
degree to which aesthetic value is seen as a fluctuating entity that draws
its existence from its constant movement along a complex circuit of
ideological relations. In contrast, aesthetic value for Bloch, although
surely conditioned by historical circumstances which the critic must
always take into account, ultimately can be discerned and judged accord-
ing to utopian knowledge. And while utopian knowledge is likewise
historically conditioned (how else could it make a claim to Marxist
"science"?), as an enduring surplus it stands outside of the false con-
sciousness of ideology—which is to say it stands both inside and outside
of history. In short, the utopian function is not relational, and in many
quarters today that is enough to prove its inadequacy.

But would Eagleton himself concur? "In what sense, if any," he asks,
"do elements of the historically 'real' enter the text?" Here is his re-
sponse:

> Ideology is not just the bad dream of the infrastructure: in *defor-
> matively* "producing" the real, it nevertheless carries elements of reality
> with it. . . . The real is by necessity empirically imperceptible, con-
> cealing itself from the phenomenal categories (commodity, wage-rela-
> tion, exchange-value and so on) it offers spontaneously for inspection.
> Ideology, rather, so produces and constructs the real as to cast the
> shadow of its absence over the perception of its presence.[11]

Eagleton's treatment of the "real" as a relatively imperceptible category
that is deformatively produced by ideology's engagement with the text is
strikingly similar to Bloch's treatment of utopian or anticipatory il-
lumination. Both the utopian and the real exist within phenomenal
categories and present themselves to us via ideological deformation.
Both are, in this respect, shadows of an absence cast over a misleading
perception of a presence.

This is not to say, however, that Marxism as a discursive practice
should be deterred from the use of such categories. As observers and
critics of culture, we inevitably hypostatize our mental experiences of
material production. The results are such essentially metaphysical but

nonetheless real notions as ideology, utopia—and the real itself. As Derrida says (and as usual, his words when applied to this case are both a warning and a consolation), *"There is no sense* in doing without the concepts of metaphysics in order to attack metaphysics. We have no language—no syntax and no lexicon—which is alien to this history; we cannot utter a single destructive proposition which has not already slipped into the form, the logic, and the implicit postulations of precisely what it seeks to contest."[12] Instead, we must recognize that since we cannot step outside of (ideological) language, we must continually transform and refine our vocabularies in the hope of achieving a greater working knowledge of cultural production. In this light, Bloch's efforts can be understood as a great contribution to our understanding of art and literature as ongoing, self-subsisting historical activities.

Bloch's writing on art and literature is itself representative of that which it continually seeks. But if this is the case, we must also note, along with Fredric Jameson, that

> The Utopian moment is indeed in one sense quite impossible for us to imagine, except as the unimaginable; thus a kind of allegorical structure is built into the very forward movement of the Utopian impulse itself, which always points to something other, which can never reveal itself directly but must always speak in figures, which always calls out structurally for completion and exegesis.[13]

This is why Jameson, in explaining Bloch's interpretive methods, invokes Paul Ricoeur's distinction between a hermeneutics of suspicion and a hermeneutics of restoration, stressing Bloch's affinity with the latter.[14] The utopian function never ceases, however, and Jameson's brilliant discussion of Bloch should be amended to stress the radical openness of Bloch's interpretations. In Bloch's ontology, "the world is full of the 'not yet' which strains as tendency."[15] It is the tendency in a process that drives it forward while at the same time indicating the incompleteness of every step along the way. Bloch's interpretive methods, therefore, do not really aim for the structural completion of a primary figure, however allegorically it may present itself. Rather, like the deconstructionist's endless play of signifiers (which Bloch would surely understand as a utopian allegory of incompletion), the process of Bloch's hermeneutics cannot seal the text, for the utopian moment as it stands revealed is that very moment when the text most strenuously resists thematic or interpretive closure. Bloch's militant optimism (which may appear to some as too cloying) compels an important distinction between the text that has been illuminated by anticipation and that which has been deconstructed: the latter plunges us into the abyss, while the former sets us on an ascending course; the latter threatens the complete negation of meaning, while the former promises an endless bounty of signification.

This binary opposition, however, requires further consideration. Just as restorative and suspicious hermeneutics are themselves implicated in one another (for the restoration of a text depends upon the preceding suspicion that it needs completion, and suspicion arises only out of a fear that all has already been restored), so, too, a utopian function characterized by plenitude and ascension cannot be regarded as distinct from a deconstruction known for a constant deferral of meaning and loss of ground. Revelations of the utopian moment in ideologically deformed cultural productions always involve a double reading of loss and gain, a simultaneity of effects, since for Bloch, "Marxism is the weapon that first gives the imagination a guilty conscience and also the same weapon that heals the affected imagination."[16] And as for deconstruction, if revelations of verbal groundlessness require violent demonstrations of the instability of signification, then they likewise involve virtual celebrations of the utopian potential of textuality as usually summed up in the notion of free play.

Thus, when Bloch confronts cultural production as what Jameson rightly calls "an immense storehouse of figures,"[17] the utopian bounty of meaning can be only *partially* unveiled in the critical act, for such plenitude is always *latent* (another important term for Bloch) in culture. All figures are prefigurative. For Bloch, the utopian function "draws images from the still valid past insofar as they are ambiguously fit for the future, despite all the spells within them, and it makes these images useful since they are the expression of what has still not happened."[18] Here, as in the later work of Walter Benjamin, we can observe traces of what could be called a kabbalistic Marxism at work. Critics continue to debate the exact relationship between Marxism and mysticism in Benjamin's work, but I would argue that for Bloch, Kabbalah (especially the Kabbalah of Isaac Luria, the sixteenth-century mystic of Safed), bearing as it does a strong messianic charge, actually may be read as a systematic prefiguration of the Marxist dialectic.

Bloch's kabbalistic Marxism is best understood in its historical context, though it also requires an actual comparison to Kabbalah and other forms of traditional Jewish textuality which can only be sketched herein.[19] In his highly informative article on Bloch and Benjamin, Anson Rabinbach uncovers

a different kind of modern Jewishness which stands under the sign of Messianism. The Messianic stance rejects religiosity, the rational and secular Judaism of the middle classes, and the personal Judaism of "renewal" represented by Martin Buber. Messianism demands a complete repudiation of the world as it is, placing its hope in a future whose realization can only be brought about by the destruction of the old order. Apocalyptic, catastrophic, utopian and pessimistic, Messianism captured a generation of Jewish intellectuals before the First World War.[20]

Given the metaphysical qualities of Bloch's hermeneutics described above, it is particularly telling that Rabinbach sees the messianic impulse as "secular *and* theological, as a tradition that stands opposed to both secular rationalism and what has been called 'normative Judaism.'"[21] The political manifestations of the messianic *ethos* vary: compare Bloch's and (eventually) Benjamin's syncretic Marxism with the Zionism of Gershom Scholem, the great historian of Jewish mysticism.[22] But it must also be remembered that "esoteric messianism" can be understood in itself "as a form of politics—as a politics against politics in the prewar and war epochs."[23] For some of the most prominent German Jewish intellectuals who came of age during World War I, messianism precedes and to a great extent determines their more overt critical stances and political decisions.

Scholem strongly disliked Bloch's first book, *The Spirit of Utopia*, especially its treatment of Judaism and its "amalgamation of Jewish Kabbalistic and Christian motifs."[24] Years later, however, in a footnote to his crucial essay on Jewish messianism, Scholem has this to say about Bloch and the utopian aspect of messianism:

> Although many of Bloch's suggestions elicit great reservations, one must admire the energy and insight with which he has approached and carried through his discussion of utopianism. The elaborate Marxist montage of his second work [*The Principle of Hope*] stands in poorly concealed contradiction to the mystical inspiration which is basically responsible for Bloch's best insights. Not without a measure of courage, he has managed to draw his insights safely through a veritable jungle of Marxist rhapsodies.[25]

It is well worth noting that despite Scholem's prejudiced attitude toward Marxism, he recognizes and applauds Bloch's essentially kabbalistic insights. If we take a more dialectical perspective and consider Bloch's Marxism not merely in contradiction to his Kabbalism but in some ways complementing it, we can see the extent to which these two messianic and utopian discourses interact in Bloch's work.

The Lurianic myth of catastrophe creation (recently popularized in the work of Harold Bloom) involves a threefold movement of limitation, destruction, and reparation, a cosmic process in which human as well as divine powers participate and which reach completion only through a long and ultimately messianic struggle for universal restoration. Creation begins with *tsimtsum*, God's withdrawal or contraction into Himself to leave a space for that which is other than pure deity. The subsequent act of emanation results in catastrophe, for the "vessels" prepared to receive the divine potencies break, dispersing God's light. According to Scholem,

> henceforth nothing is perfect. The divine light which should have subsisted in specific forms and in places appointed for it from the beginning is no longer in its proper place because the vessels were broken, and thereafter all things went awry. Nothing is in the place appointed for it; everything is either below or above, but not where it should be. In other words, all being is in Gault [exile].[26]

The notion that deity itself exists in a state of exile which is both analogous to and the ultimate cause of the exile of the Jewish people casts Jewish law and custom into a purely messianic light. Because the sparks of divine light are dispersed in a universe of evil and impurity (worsened, for humanity, by the "second fall" of Adam in the Garden of Eden), it is up to the Jewish people, through their daily religious observances, to "lift up the sparks" and hasten the process of *tikkun,* or cosmic restoration.

When this process is reinterpreted by Bloch as an intellectual praxis in the field of secular culture, the result is some of his most uncanny theoretrical utterances. Consider this astonishing formulation:

> The course of the world is still undecided, unended, and so is the depth in all aesthetic information: *this utopian element is the paradox in the aesthetic immanence. . . .* For the world itself, as it lies in malice, lies in incompleteness and in the experimental process away from malice. The figures that this process generates, the ciphers, the allegories, and the symbols, in which the process is so rich, are *altogether fragments, real-fragments themselves through which the process flows unevenly and through which the process proceeds dialectically toward further forms of fragments.*[27]

This is a restorative hermeneutic inspired by the concept of *tikkun.* Like the kabbalist who believes that the proper *mitzvot* (good deeds) will raise the sparks of the fallen worlds and hasten universal healing, Bloch puts his hope in the incompleteness of the cultural process. From this perspective, cultural production consists of shards waiting to be raised to a utopian state through the *mitzvah* of criticism (or revolution) and requiring a materialist understanding of aesthetics.

We are now in a better position to understand why for Habermas, "Bloch's basic experience is darkness,"[28] an assertion that applies both to Bloch's conceptual framework and to his style. Entering "Better Castles in the Sky at the County Fair and Circus, in Fairy Tales and Colportage" (the trip begins with the title), readers find themselves rapidly skating across sheets of fantasy imagery, encountering fragments of plots, catalogs of types and figures, arrays of historical and generic categories and distinctions. But in the midst of such broad surveys, singular trenchant statements abruptly impose themselves, as when Bloch stops doubling the texts to remind us that "the fairy tale does not presume to be a substitute for action."[29] The endless projection of encyclopedic references, the rhetorical equivalent of Bloch's relentless utopian quest, is counterbalanced by his darkened, opaque passages, suddenly illuminated. Likewise, in "A Philosophical View of the Detective Novel," Bloch is not merely content to trace the popular genre back to its roots in some of the earliest great works of literature, such as *Oedipus*. Following his kabbalistic model, he takes the detective plot back before Genesis, interpreting the Lurianic notion of *tsimtsum* as a kind of "capture," a self-kidnapping by God.[30] The result is darkness, the abyss as *incognito* upon which the world is founded. Thus, as we probe the present moment, we are part rationalistic detective, part mystic, sifting through the fragments for some clue to the original act of inspiration. As Benjamin would say, "origin is the goal."

Unfortunately, Bloch's investigations occasionally led him astray, his political judgments taking on a dark cast that is downright insidious compared to any opacity of style. Even the most sympathetic of Bloch's readers must deal with the troubling contradictions in his attitudes and pronouncements regarding official Communist ideology, especially after he returned to East Germany from exile in the United States in 1949. Bloch's defense of Stalinism and his blanket condemnations of "fascist America," both in personal statements and in *The Principle of Hope*, conflict with what Jack Zipes calls Bloch's "great emphasis on creative experimentation and the *unfinished* nature of the socialist project."[31] Such contradictions eventually led to Bloch's move to West Germany in 1961 after increasingly harsh and repressive treatment by East German authorities. As with the equally checkered career of Georg Lukács, it is important to consider such historical vicissitudes, while at the same time posing a more complex set of questions about the man and his work: What is the relationship between the theoretical system of the critic and his concrete intellectual decisions? To what extent are we to judge the former in the light of the latter? How does the nature of the theory itself affect our expectations when the work and the life are assessed in these terms?

Bloch's utopianism imposes difficult conditions upon those who invest in it. Just as hope is always thwarted and utopian fulfillment is always latent, both struggling under the stern sign of the "not yet," so specific acts, statements, and decisions are to be regarded as provisional and incomplete. As Wayne Hudson observes in his explication of Bloch's metaphysics, "we do not see the moment in which we live: there is an invisibility at the heart of our existence."[32] This is in no way meant to be understood as a standing excuse for failures of judgment: what Bloch calls "losses on the march forward" are real losses, not "dialectical" sublations to airbrushed out of history by the propaganda department, like the figure of Clementis in Milan Kundera's *Book of Laughter and Forgetting*. In this respect, Bloch's sense of tragedy, despite his constant optimism, shows him to be a true "Western Marxist." On the other hand, those who labor in the spirit of utopia, creating what Marx calls "the poetry of the future," understand the inevitability of their failures and the necessity of revision—not in the manner of the opportunist, but in the manner, indeed, of the poet constantly seeking *le mot juste*. I think this is the way to understand Bloch's "Stalinism"; and it should be remembered that when he finally got a true taste of it (he was sixty-three in 1948, never having held a teaching post, when the University of Leipzig offered him the chair of philosophy), he struggled against it until he was forced to retreat to the West. And unlike Lukács, whose failure to comprehend modernism was certainly due in part to his dogmatic Communism, Bloch, in his aesthetic assessments, rarely suffered from his failures of political vision, as seen in his advocacy of Kafka and Brecht and the fascinating influence of expressionism on his own writing style.

The most telling critique of Bloch's theories, if it is to be found, lies in what someone like Kundera might call Bloch's "lyric attitude." Kundera describes the Stalinist period as "not only an epoch of terror, but also an epoch of lyricism, ruled hand in hand by the hangman and the poet,"[33] an insight that led to his expulsion as a young man from the Czech Communist party in 1948. Considering the betrayal of the Czech surrealist Zavis Kalandra by Paul Eluard, Kundera also observes: "when an executioner kills, that is after all normal; but when a poet (and a great poet) sings in accompaniment, the whole system of values we considered sacrosanct has suddenly been shaken apart. Nothing is certain any longer. Everything turns problematic, questionable, subject of analysis and doubt: Progress and Revolution. Youth. Motherhood. Even Man. And also Poetry."[34]

Much earlier, in 1935, when Nazi domination was spreading and communism (including its Stalinist form) in Central Europe was virtually inconceivable, Bloch writes a brief but crucial essay called "Marxism and Poetry." This essay addresses the problem of the poet who, although strongly sympathetic to Marxism, feels that Marxist criticism precludes the individual experience of inwardness that produces lyricism and the poetic aura. What will occur when one attempts to reconcile the lyric attitude with Marxism? Bloch's treatment of the matter is as unsettling as Kundera's:

if one chooses to accept Marxism, then it opens gates to poetry where the bleakness, solitude and disorientation of late capitalism are pressing concerns. It shows movement and landscape being newly formed that lose nothing of their abundance and aspirations through exact topography. Instead of sterility and the non-existence of problems . . . Marxism shows countless problems of motion and incompleteness within a reality whose tendency and utopian backgrounds require more geniuses to express it than there are muses.[35]

In short, for the Marxist poet, "the imagination is no longer a social outcast."[36]

The ironies are manifold. One can almost see Bloch putting his arms around the shoulders of some youthful comrades and joining in Kundera's insidious circle dance, "the gigantic ring encircling Paris, Moscow, Warsaw, Prague, Sofia, and Athens, encircling all the socialist countries and all the Communist parties of the world."[37] Yet, in the same essay, Bloch tells us that Marxism can provide access to the *"subject pending in process,"* "access to poetry that has nothing in common with self-satisfaction and illusion."[38] Clearly we are in the presence of a critic who has true insight into the poetic process, who understands the ongoing necessity of conceiving of poetry as an aesthetic production of the subject, which in turn maintains the subject's integrity through perpetual flux and change.

Maintaining such integrity may seem like a quaint Romantic holdover in Bloch's thought, especially from the hegemonic perspective of today's Postmodernism. As Jameson has argued, Postmodernism in theoretical and artistic work abandons intellectual "depth models," including "the dialectical one of essence and appearance," replacing them with the affectless play of surfaces.[39] In contrast, Bloch believes that "the poetical depiction of the essential is based on something fundamental that does not appear at all so clearly in the empirical substance or has not become obvious in any way whatsoever. The subjective factor of the poetical is then the midwife of the artistic anticipatory illumination."[40] Bloch's understanding of poetry as a practice of essences by a centered human subject is not purely a matter of Romantic idealism. It is effectively refunctioned by his unique version of Marxism, in which poetic subjectivity aids in the birth of "anticipatory illumination" within the empirical substance of the text. On the other hand, when Bloch speaks of process, it is not merely the indiscriminate openness which leads us, as Jameson points out, to the fragmentation of the subject and the resultant free-floating and impersonal euphoria that pervades contemporary writing and art.[41] Arguably, Bloch's conception of the poetic process plots a course midway between an idealization of the subject and its total dismemberment. As Bloch understands it, "meaningful poetry makes the world become aware of an *accelerated flow of action,* an *elucidating waking dream of the essential.* The world wants to be changed in this way.

Therefore, the *correlate of the world* to the poetically appropriate action is precisely the *tendency*. The poetically appropriate waking dream is precisely the *latency* of existence."[42]

It is hard to miss the Hegelian inflection here, and a steady diet of such pronouncements may soon have one longing for the more recent awareness of the materiality of the signifier. Be that as it may, Bloch's view of poetry is not to be slighted. As a crucial site for the apprehension of material change, the poetic subject elucidates, through rarefied linguistic production, what we can only perceive as a waking dream—a notion that is remarkably similar to Pound's remark that "poets are the antennae of the race." Thus poetry, like dreams (or nightmares), calls for interpretation and an extreme sensitivity to the tendency and latency encoded in the text. And because both poets and interpreters live in history, their work can only be conditional: their truth is always pending.

According to Bloch, "the works of culture arise strategically";[43] there is very little that is fortuitous about them. Yet these strategies are in constant flux. This partly accounts for Bloch's concepts of tendency and latency, especially as they apply to the judgment of newly emergent works, but also in reconsidering those works that have already been deemed canonical. As I argued in chap. 1, Bloch's theories are of great importance to the study of canon formation: the work's utopian function, articulated by the critic in a moment of anticipatory illumination, serves as one of our greatest weapons against the gross facticity of consumer capitalism, or more generally, what Benjamin called, with his gloomy prescience, *das Immergleich*, the ever-the-same. Against a value-neutral play of Postmodern surfaces *and* a reified, monumental worship of the past, we may place Bloch's view of cultural heritage, which "disdains that which has been called famous in its own time without due reason, disconnects that which has been famous in its own time with good reason based on evidence from the ideology of that time and now continually fills it with the true evidence of its implications."[44] What promise does the work make to futurity? The question is admittedly perilous given our finite historical being, but it remains indispensable to any act of cultural evaluation. No matter how ponderous or abstract his answers may be, Ernst Bloch has confronted this question more directly and intelligently than any other modern critic.

In a seminal essay on Frederic Jameson (who introduced American criticism to Bloch in *Marxism and Form*), Terry Eagleton claims that "in dealing with Hegel or Northrop Frye, it seems less important to interrogate the contents of their systems than to indicate the historical appropriateness of the systems themselves, their formal status within history."[45] No doubt Eagleton would call for precisely the same treatment of Bloch, paying special attention to his utopian hermeneutic not merely as an interpretation of culture but as a highly determined cultural production, whose appropriateness—that most withering of Marxist terms, often used by Bloch himself—must be scrupulously judged according to its historical circumstances. In response to such latter-day Marxist foxes, Bloch the hedgehog could say only that his system is *not yet* appropriate; the utopian refunctioning of Marxism, like Kafka's messiah, will be appropriate only when it is no longer necessary for it to be so. In other words, the "historical inappropriateness" of a theory is a good sign of its ultimate importance.

Notes

Introduction: On Methodology

1. Kenneth Burke, *A Grammar of Motives and a Rhetoric of Motives* (Cleveland, Ohio: World Publishing Co., 1962), 506.
2. Fredric Jameson, *Marxism and Form* (Princeton: Princeton University Press, 1971), 110–11.
3. Terry Eagleton, "Fredric James: The Politics of Style," *Diacritics* 12, no. 3 (Fall 1982): 21. Also consider this remark: "The vulnerability of Western Marxism to idealist deformation lies above all in its relative separation from mass revolutionary practice; and the fate of most 'Marxist aesthetics' has been to reproduce this condition at a specific level." Terry Eagleton, *Walter Benjamin or towards a Revolutionary Criticism* (London: NLB, 1981), 82.
4. Karl Marx and Friedrich Engels, *The German Ideology*, ed. C. J. Arthur (New York: International Publishers, 1970), especially 46–48. I am grateful to Henry Weinfield, who helped me clarify these observations.
5. Cliff Slaughter, *Marxism, Ideology and Literature* (Atlantic Highlands, N.J.: Humanities Press, 1980), 46.
6. Ibid., 85. For Slaughter's full-fledged refutation of Eagleton, see 201–10.
7. Gerald Graff, *Literature against Itself: Literary Ideas in Modern Society* (Chicago: University of Chicago Press, 1979), 23–24.
8. Gerald Graff, letter to the editors, *American Book Review* 3, no. 4 (May/June 1981): 2.
9. Jameson, *Marxism and Form*, 119–20.
10. Walter Benjamin, *Illuminations*, trans. Harry Zohn (New York: Schocken Books, 1968), 263.

Chapter 1. At the Front: Evaluating Contemporary Poetry

1. James E. Breslin, *From Modern to Contemporary: American Poetry 1945–1965* (Chicago: University of Chicago Press, 1984), 250.
2. Ibid., 255.
3. Robert Von Hallberg, *American Poetry and Culture 1945–1980* (Cambridge: Harvard University Press, 1985), 228.
4. Charles Altieri, *Self and Sensibility in Contemporary American Poetry* (Cambridge: Cambridge University Press, 1984), 6.
5. Ibid., 19.
6. Charles Newman, *The Post-Modern Aura: The Act of Fiction in an Age of Inflation* (Evanston, Ill.: Northwestern University Press, 1985), 6.
7. Ibid., 46.

8. Ibid., 123.

9. Ibid., 125.

10. Altieri, *Self and Sensibility*, 73.

11. Alan Williamson, *Introspection and Contemporary Poetry* (Cambridge: Harvard University Press, 1984), 96.

12. Von Hallberg, *American Poetry and Culture*, 28.

13. Newman, *Post-Modern Aura*, 13.

14. Wayne Hudson, *The Marxist Philosophy of Ernst Bloch* (New York: St. Martin's Press, 1982), 116.

15. Ernst Bloch, *A Philosophy of the Future*, trans. John Cumming (New York: Herder and Herder, 1970), 144.

16. Ibid., 95.

17. Fredric Jameson, *The Political Unconscious* (Ithaca: Cornell University Press, 1981), 291. In this regard, also consider Charles Altieri's declaration that "Emancipation depends on correlating the negative critical work of demystification with the positive models and powers we can locate in culturally preserved forms of idealization," in "An Idea and Ideal of a Literary Canon," in *Canons*, ed. Robert Von Hallberg (Chicago: University of Chicago Press, 1984), 49.

18. Terry Eagleton, *Criticism and Ideology* (London: NLB, 1976), 98–99.

19. Frank E. and Fritzie P. Manuel, *Utopian Thought in the Western World* (Cambridge: Harvard University Press, 1979), 5.

20. Gerald L. Bruns, "Canon and Power in the Hebrew Scriptures," in *Canons*, 81, 67.

21. Altieri, *Self and Sensibility*, 8.

22. Von Hallberg, *American Poetry and Culture*, 27.

23. Christine Froula, "When Eve Reads Milton: Undoing the Canonical Economy," in *Canons*, 151.

24. Eagleton, *Criticism and Ideology*, 56–57.

25. Von Hallberg, *American Poetry and Culture*, 27–28.

26. Hans Robert Jauss, *Toward an Aesthetic of Reception*, trans. Timothy Bahti (Minneapolis: University of Minnesota Press, 1982), 35.

27. Ibid., 26.

28. W. B. Yeats, *Essays and Introductions* (New York: Macmillan, 1961), 111.

29. *The Collected Books of Jack Spicer*, ed. Robin Blaser (Los Angeles: Black Sparrow Press, 1975), 179.

30. Theodor Adorno, *Prisms*, trans. Samuel and Shierry Weber (Cambridge: MIT Press, 1981), 23.

31. See Fredric Jameson's discussion of the commoditization of contemporary art in *Marxism and Form* (Princeton: Princeton University Press, 1971), 413–15.

32. William Bronk, *Life Supports: New and Collected Poems* (San Francisco: North Point Press, 1981), 120.

33. See Georg Lukács, *The Theory of the Novel*, trans. Anna Bostock (Cambridge: MIT Press, 1971), 114. In the Anglo-American tradition, the study that best complements Lukács's analysis is Frank Kermode, *Romantic Image* (New York: Vintage Books, 1957), 1–29.

34. See Charles Altieri, "The Objectivist Tradition," *Chicago Review* 30, no. 3 (Winter 1979): 5–22, for the most well-known attempt to distinguish this tradition from historical antecedents and contemporary alternatives. Although I do not agree with all of Altieri's distinctions, the essay is a good introduction to what remains, for the most part, our present situation. Since 1982, *Sagetrieb*, "a journal devoted to poets in the Pound-H.D.-Williams tradition," has sought to codify and delineate this strain. See especially Don Byrd, "The Poetry of Production,"

Sagetrieb 2, no. 2 (Summer/Fall 1983): 7–43, which, despite its rather jaundiced view of Marxian utopias (13–14), provides a provocative summary of the philosophical as well as literary preconditions of this crucial body of poetry.

35. George Oppen, *Collected Poems* (New York: New Directions, 1975), 168.

Chapter 2. What Was Objectivism?

1. William Carlos Williams, *Selected Essays* (New York: New Directions, 1954), 212.

2. Benjamin, *Illuminations*, 223–24. Also see 83–109, 155–94.

3. William Carlos Williams, *Imaginations*, ed. Webster Schott (New York: New Directions, 1970), 120.

4. Hugh Kenner, *A Homemade World* (New York: Knopf, 1975), 70.

5. Oppen, *Collected Poems*, 157.

6. *Collected Earlier Poems of William Carlos Williams* (New York: New Directions, 1951), 88–89.

7. Robert Von Hallberg, "The Politics of Description: W. C. Williams in the 'Thirties," *ELH* 45 (1978): 131.

8. Oppen, *Collected Poems*, 160.

9. Williams, *Imaginations*, 117.

10. *Prepositions: The Collected Critical Essays of Louis Zukofsky* (Berkeley: University of California Press, 1981), 12.

11. Ibid., 13.

12. In his essay on the Objectivist tradition, Charles Altieri correctly identifies sincerity as a basis for Objectivist composition. However, he relates the concept to "refusing the temptation of closure—both closure as fixed form and closure as writing in the service of idea, doctrine, or abstract aesthetic ideal." Obviously, I disagree that sincerity precludes such acts of closure, for the idea of sincerity itself is historically conditioned, and has been proven flexible enough to be made manifest in numerous forms and conceptual systems within the poem. See Altieri, "The Objectivist Tradition," 14–15. Hugh Kenner also considers Zukofsky's use of sincerity and objectification, but like Altieri, does not consider the notion of perfection in the elaboration of Zukofsky's poetic stance. See Kenner, *A Homemade World*, 165–67.

13. Oppen, *Collected Poems*, 172.

14. George Oppen, in *The Contemporary Writer*, ed. L. S. Dembo and Cyrena N. Pondrom (Madison: University of Wisconsin Press, 1972), 174.

15. Charles Olson, *Human Universe & Other Essays*, ed. Donald Allen (New York: Grove Press, 1967), 56.

16. Bloch, *A Philosophy of the Future*, 91.

17. Louis Zukofsky, *All: The Collected Short Poems* (New York: Norton, 1971), 120.

18. For an examination of Williams's relation to Keats and its effect on Objectivist poetics, see Norman Finkelstein, "Beauty, Truth and *The Wanderer*," in *William Carlos Williams: Man & Poet*, ed. C. F. Terrell (Orono, Maine: National Poetry Foundation, 1983), 233–42.

19. See Peter Quartermain, " 'Not At All Surprised By Science': Louis Zukofsky's *First Half of "A"-9*," in *Louis Zukofsky: Man & Poet*, ed. C. F. Terrell (Orono, Maine: National Poetry Foundation, 1979), 203–25, for a more complete examination of the poem's sources.

20. Louis Zukofsky, *"A"* (Berkeley: University of California Press, 1978), 110.

21. Ibid., 107.

22. Ibid., 111.

23. Oppen, *Collected Poems*, 150.

24. Ibid., 151.

25. Ibid., 174.

26. Cf. Norman Finkelstein, "Syntax and Tradition: George Oppen's *Primitive*," in *George Oppen: Man and Poet*, ed. Burton Hatlen (Orono, Maine: National Poetry Foundation, 1981), 429–44.

27. Zukofsky, *"A"*, 536.

28. Barry Ahearn says that in exploring the intellectual content of *"A"-22* and *23*, "the mind slips into the soothing care of that anesthetic cadence. Zukofsky may well have planned this brain-frustrating strategy to insure that a single reading of the movements could only be carried on at the musical level. Those merely intellectual faculties would have to be content with a piecemeal apprehension." I appreciate Ahearn's ambitious first reading of *"A"*, but I must disagree here: Zukofsky, more than any other recent poet, foregrounds the musicality of meaning, but still relies on meaningful syntax to so great an extent that it seems unlikely that two such crucial movements are meant to be read finally for their music alone. See Barry Ahearn, *Zukofsky's "A"* (Berkeley: University of California Press, 1983), 181.

29. Hyatt H. Waggoner, *American Visionary Poetry* (Baton Rouge: Louisiana State University Press, 1982), 7. Waggoner includes Williams among his visionaries in a well-reasoned chapter (89–111) which does, however, sell Williams short in terms of the number of successful poems he has produced.

30. Oppen, *Collected Poems*, 185.

31. Robert Creeley, *A Quick Graph: Collected Notes & Essays*, ed. Donald Allen (San Francisco: Four Seasons Foundation, 1970), 19.

Chapter 3. O'Hara, Ashbery, and the Loss of the Sublime

1. Linking Ashbery and O'Hara in a critical discussion has become something of a risk, given the recent reactions to the convenient appellation of the "New York School." While I fully recognize the important differences between the two poets and examine some of them in the following pages, my work here still turns on the idea that both poets participate in what has become an ongoing poetic project with shared strategies and one ideological base.

2. Charles Molesworth, *The Fierce Embrace* (Columbia: University of Missouri Press, 1979), 95.

3. See, especially, Marjorie Perloff, *Frank O'Hara: Poet among Painters* (New York: George Braziller, 1977), 125–39 and passim; and *The Poetry of Indeterminacy* (Princeton: Princeton University Press, 1981), 249–87.

4. John Ashbery, *Rivers and Mountains* (New York: Holt Rinehart Winston, 1966), 39.

5. Kenneth Burke, *The Philosophy of Literary Form*, 2d ed. (Baton Rouge: Louisiana State University Press, 1967), 61.

6. Molesworth, *Fierce Embrace*, 92–97, 180–81.

7. Graff, *Literature against Itself*, 118–19.

8. See Douglas Crase, "The Prophetic Ashbery" and Keith Cohen, "Ashbery's Dismantling of Bourgeois Discourse," in *Beyond Amazement: New Essays on John Ashbery*, ed. David Lehman (Ithaca: Cornell University Press, 1980), 30–65 and 128–49.

9. Harold Bloom, *Figures of Capable Imagination* (New York: Seabury Press,

1976), 179. In examining Ashbery in relation to the sublime, I am obviously following Bloom's lead. However, Bloom's idealization of Ashbery, which seems necessary given the inherent strictures of his system—"strong" poets must somehow survive, if for no other reason than for "strong" critics to canonize them—overlooks some of the poet's serious shortcomings. These are shortcomings which Ashbery shares with O'Hara, who, for some unnamed reason, Bloom must consider a "weaker" poet.

10. *The Collected Poems of Frank O'Hara*, ed. Donald Allen (New York: Knopf, 1971), 500.

11. John Ashbery, *Self-Portrait in a Convex Mirror* (New York: Penguin, 1975), 2.

12. See, for example, the highly idealized response to the poem in Lawrence Lieberman, *Unassigned Frequencies* (Urbana: University of Illinois Press, 1977), 3–61.

13. As Don Byrd says, "Ashbery's preeminence among contemporary American poets is in a sense deserved: it has fallen to him to carry one of the most honored cultural strategies to its final extreme. After Ashbery, it is completely possible to continue along linguistic *detours* which lead to symbolic representations of inanimate integrity, but the journey itself becomes tedious, and so little vitality is left in the cliches (however twisted or ironically misapplied) that it is hard to feel personally involved. One becomes a voyeur to one's most intimate processes." Don Byrd, "The Poetry of Production," 25.

14. John Ashbery, "An Interview in Warsaw," in *Code of Signals: Recent Writings in Poetics*, ed. Michael Palmer (Berkeley: North Atlantic Books, 1983), 307–8.

15. O'Hara, *Collected Poems*, 350–51.

16. O'Hara's tone in this poem is certainly under control, but at his weaker moments, what Trotsky says of Mayakovsky could apply equally well to him: "Mayakovsky shouts too often, where he should merely speak; that is why his shouting, in those places where he ought to shout, seems insufficient." Leon Trotsky, *Literature and Revolution*, trans. Rose Strunsky (Ann Arbor: University of Michigan Press, 1960), 151. Many of Trotsky's remarks about the Futurists, especially their use of form, are worth considering in regard to O'Hara.

17. See Molesworth, *Fierce Embrace*, 164, and Perloff, *Frank O'Hara*, 190–95.

18. Charles Altieri, *Enlarging the Temple* (Lewisburg, Pa.: Bucknell University Press, 1979), 119.

19. Breslin, *Modern to Contemporary*, 217.

20. Ibid., 211.

21. O'Hara, *Collected Poems*, 167.

22. O'Hara may be playing, however unconsciously, with the first stanza of Stevens's poem "The American Sublime":

> How does one stand
> To behold the sublime,
> To confront the mockers,
> The mickey mockers
> And plaited pairs?

If such is the case, O'Hara might wish for a version of the American sublime ("And the sublime comes down / To the spirit itself"), but could never be satisfied with it—as it true for Stevens himself in his greatest poems.

23. O'Hara, *Collected Poems*, 217.

24. *The Collected Poems of Wallace Stevens* (New York: Knopf, 1954), 326.

25. See Perloff, *Frank O'Hara*, 141–46 and Alan Feldman, *Frank O'Hara* (Boston: Twayne, 1979), 92–97.

26. Breslin, *Modern to Contemporary*, 243.

27. O'Hara, *Collected Poems*, 256–57.

28. Feldman, *Frank O'Hara*, 37.

29. O'Hara, *Collected Poems*, 281.

30. Sigmund Freud, *Civilization and Its Discontents*, Vol. 21 (1927–31) in *The Standard Edition of the Complete Works of Sigmund Freud*, trans. James Strachey (London: The Hogarth Press, 1961), 141.

31. As Alan Williamson notes, Ashbery is "a poet whom each of his admirers is likely to have a strong desire to rescue from some of the others"—though he does not offer an explicit reason for this situation. See Williamson, *Introspection*, 116.

32. Jameson, *Marxism and Form*, 343.

33. Williamson, *Introspection*, 119.

34. Ibid., 120, 117.

35. Ibid., 137.

36. John Ashbery, *The Double Dream of Spring* (New York: Dutton, 1970), 33.

37. John Ashbery, *Some Trees* (1956; reprint, New York: Ecco Press, 1978), 23.

38. Ashbery, *Rivers and Mountains*, 9.

39. When I had the opportunity to meet Ashbery and tell him of my admiration for this poem, he informed me that he had the cities of Switzerland in mind when he wrote it. Given their roles as centers of finance and havens for exiled artists and intellectuals, they are the ideal models for the lacustrine cities he describes.

40. David Rigsbee, "Against Monuments: A Reading of Ashbery's 'These Lacustrine Cities,'" in *Beyond Amazement*, 209–23. Much of what Rigsbee says of the poem is certainly accurate, but I cannot share with him the notion that it is a thoroughgoing critique of the "will-to-monument." Williamson, on the other hand, recognizes Ashbery's ambivalence toward the project of civilization in his useful remarks on the poem. See Williamson, *Introspection*, 138–40.

41. Cf. Herbert Marcuse: "The flux of time is society's most natural ally in maintaining law and order, conformity, and the institutions that relegate freedom to a perpetual utopia; the flux of time helps men to forget what was and what can be: it makes them oblivious to the better past and the better future." *Eros and Civilization* (Boston: Beacon Press, 1966), 231.

42. Ashbery, *Self-Portrait*, 19.

43. John Ashbery, *As We Know* (New York: Penguin, 1979), 93.

44. Ibid., 96.

45. Cf. Jack Spicer's treatment of the same theme—a theme that comes to dominate his poetic stance—in a poem like "Cantata":

> Ridiculous
> How the space between three violins
> Can threaten all our poetry.
> We bunch together like Cub
> Scouts at a picnic. There is a high scream.
> Rain threatens. That moment of terror.
> Strange how all our beliefs
> Disappear.

46. Altieri, *Self and Sensibility,* 132.

47. Williamson, *Introspection,* 135.

48. Ashbery, *Self-Portrait,* 60.

49. Ibid., 3.

50. Ibid., 69.

51. Perloff, *Frank O'Hara,* 190.

52. John Ashbery, *Houseboat Days* (New York: Penguin, 1977), 1.

Chapter 4. The New Arcady

1. See Norman Finkelstein, "Robert Duncan, Poet of the Law," *Sagetrieb* 2, no. 1 (Spring 1983): 75–88 and "Jack Spicer's Ghosts and the Gnosis of History," *Boundary 2* 9, no. 2 (Winter 1981): 81–99, for further development of the ideas presented in this chapter. Another crucial essay that informs my view of the poets discussed herein, especially in regard to Duncan's notion of tradition and to general issues of canon formation is Michael André Bernstein, "Robert Duncan: Talent and the Individual Tradition," *Sagetrieb* 4, nos. 2 and 3 (Fall & Winter 1985): 177–90.

2. Robert Duncan, *Bending the Bow* (New York: New Directions, 1968), 79.

3. W. B. Yeats, *Mythologies* (New York: Macmillan, 1959), 336.

4. Spicer, *Collected Books,* 176.

5. Robert Duncan, *The Years as Catches* (Berkeley, Calif.: Oyez Press, 1966), 83.

6. Spicer, *Collected Books,* 179.

7. Ibid., 15.

8. Consider various remarks in Shelley's *A Defense of Poetry,* Yeats's *A General Introduction for My Work,* Pound's *Literary Essays* and Eliot's *Tradition and the Individual Talent.*

9. Robert Duncan, *Fictive Certainties* (New York: New Directions, 1985), 28.

10. Ibid., 17–18. Cf. these remarks as well: "Every particular is an immediate happening of meaning at large; every present activity in the poem redistributes future as well as past events. This is a presence extended in a time we create as we keep words in mind." Duncan, *Bending the Bow,* ix.

11. Jack Spicer, "Excerpts from the Vancouver Lectures," in *The Poetics of the New American Poetry,* ed. Donald Allen and Warren Tallman (New York: Grove, 1973), 228.

12. Ernst Bloch, *Man on His Own,* trans. E. B. Ashton (New York: Herder and Herder, 1970), 83.

13. Duncan, *Fictive Certainties,* 33.

14. Duncan, *Bending the Bow,* 78.

15. Spicer, *Collected Books,* 171.

16. Ibid., 218.

17. Cf. William Bronk's poem "Of the All with Which We Co-exist":

> If I am anything at all, I am
> the instrument of the world's passion and not
> the doer or the done to. It is to feel.
> You, also, are such an instrument.

Although Bronk does not emphasize the terror of such an apprehension, his view of inspiration at this point parallels that of Spicer.

18. Spicer, *Collected Books*, 259.

19. See Nathaniel Mackey, "Uroboros: *Dante* and *A Seventeenth Century Suite*," in *Robert Duncan: Scales of the Marvelous*, ed. Robert J. Bertholf and Ian W. Reid (New York: New Directions, 1979), 181–97, for a demonstration of this idea in Duncan's later poetry.

20. Spicer, *Poetics*, 233.

21. Peter Riley, "The Narratives of *The Holy Grail*," *Boundary 2* 6, no. 1 (Fall 1977): 165.

22. Duncan, *Bending the Bow*, vii.

23. Spicer, *Collected Books*, 34.

24. Graff, *Literature against Itself*, 149.

25. Robert Duncan, *Ground Work: Before the War* (New York: New Directions, 1984), 106–7.

26. Duncan, *Fictive Certainties*, 46.

27. Duncan, *Ground Work*, 168.

28. Ibid., 167.

29. Ibid., 173.

30. Ibid., 171.

31. Ibid., 175.

32. Spicer, *Collected Books*, 188.

33. Ibid., 200.

34. Ibid., 213.

35. Ibid., 320–21.

36. Olson, *Human Universe*, 67.

37. *The English Auden*, ed. Edward Mendelson (New York: Random House, 1977), 391.

38. Don Byrd, "The Question of Wisdom as Such," in *Scales of the Marvelous*, 38–55.

39. For some considerations of the canonic implications of this revision, see reviews of the anthology by Burton Hatlen, *Sagetrieb* 1, no. 2 (Fall 1982): 325–28; and Jerome Rothenberg, "Keeping It Old: A Review of the New *New American Poetry*," *Sulfur* 6 (1983): 181–90.

40. Helen Adam, *Turn Again to Me & Other Poems* (New York: Kulchur Foundation, 1977), 109–10.

41. See Norman Finkelstein, "Helen Adam and Romantic Desire," *Credences* 3, no. 3 (Fall 1985): 125–37 for a full discussion of Adam's relation to this tradition.

42. More of Adam's background is revealed in Lita Hornick, "The Haunted Land of Helen Adam," *Sun & Moon* 9/10 (Summer 1980): 138–41.

43. Helen Adam, *Selected Poems & Ballads* (New York: Helekon Press, 1974), 17–18.

44. Dorothy Dinnerstein, *The Mermaid and the Minotaur: Sexual Arrangements and Human Malaise* (New York: Harper and Row, 1976), 146.

45. Ibid., 112.

46. Adam has refused to take a feminist stance on modern sexual relations, claiming that her belief in reincarnation obviates essential sexual differences. Her poems, however, seem to me to imply a penetrating critique of such relations, in the tradition of Freud, Marcuse and Dinnerstein; and these insights are granted in part by her arcane beliefs. See Hornick, "Haunted Land," 141.

47. Adam, *Selected Poems*, 26.

48. Ibid., 26–27.

49. Marcuse, *Eros and Civilization*, 233. Cf. that most chaste of utopian declarations, Walter Benjamin's conclusion to his *Theses on the Philosophy of History:*

We know that the Jews were prohibited from investigating the future. The Torah and the prayers instruct them in remembrance, however. This stripped the future of its magic, to which all those succumb who turn to the soothsayers for enlightenment. This does not imply, however, that for the Jews the future turned into homogeneous, empty time. For every second of time was the strait gate through which the Messiah might enter. (Benjamin, *Illuminations*, 264)

50. The situation I am describing here is also applicable to Duncan's early poetry, especially his *Medieval Scenes* and *Berkeley Poems*.

51. Adam, *Turn Again*, 24.

52. Ibid., 23.

53. Benjamin, *Illuminations*, 263.

54. William Harmon, "The Poetry of a Journal at the End of an Arbor in a Watch," *Parnassus* 9, no. 1 (Spring/Summer 1981): 217.

55. Guy Davenport, *The Geography of the Imagination* (San Francisco: North Point Press, 1981), 190–91.

56. Ronald Johnson, *The Book of the Green Man* (New York: Norton, 1967), 66.

57. Davenport, *Geography*, 191.

58. Ronald Johnson, *Valley of the Many-Colored Grasses* (New York: Norton, 1969), 18.

59. Johnson, *Book of the Green Man*, 33.

60. Johnson, *Valley*, 69.

61. Ibid., 23–24.

62. Zukofsky, *Prepositions*, 12.

63. Johnson, *Valley*, 107–8.

64. Ronald Johnson, *Radi Os* (Albany, Calif.: Sand Dollar Press, 1977), 46.

65. Johnson, *Book of the Green Man*, 19–20.

66. Ibid., 75–76.

67. Ibid., 83.

68. Ibid., 68.

69. Ibid., 80–81.

70. Ronald Johnson, *Ark: The Foundations* (San Francisco: North Point Press, 1980), n. pag. [76].

71. Johnson, *Radi Os*, 60–61.

72. Northrop Frye, *Anatomy of Criticism: Four Essays* (Princeton: Princeton University Press, 1957), 119.

73. Jameson, *Political Unconscious*, 74.

74. Helen Adam, *Gone Sailing* (West Branch, Iowa: The Toothpaste Press, 1980), n. pag. [28].

75. Ross Feld, *Plum Poems* (New York: Jargon Society, 1972), n. pag. [11].

Chapter 5. The Utopia of Language

1. Michael Davidson, *The San Francisco Renaissance* (Cambridge: Cambridge University Press, 1989), 215.

2. Spicer, *Collected Books*, 132.

3. For a detailed account of language poetry in relation to the "avant-garde tradition," see George Hartley, *Textual Politics and the Language Poets* (Bloomington: Indiana University Press, 1989), 1–25. A focused introduction to the language poets' concern with referentiality and the status of the self can be

found in Lee Bartlett, "What Is 'Language Poetry'?," *Critical Inquiry* 12, no. 4 (Summer 1986): 741–52.

4. Raymond Williams, *Marxism and Literature* (Oxford: Oxford University Press, 1977), 126.

5. Charles Bernstein, *Content's Dream: Essays 1975–1984* (Los Angeles: Sun & Moon Press, 1986), 401–2. In her groundbreaking essay "The Word as Such: L=A=N=G=U=A=G=E poetry in the eighties," Marjorie Perloff also mentions the charge that the poems of the language poets are not as interesting as their theories. Unfortunately, Perloff does not pursue the issue, but dissolves it into a more general discussion of poetry versus prose. See Marjorie Perloff, *The Dance of the Intellect* (Cambridge: Cambridge University Press, 1985), 222–23.

6. Ibid., 402.

7. I use the term "reader" in the spirit of George Steiner's essay "'Critic'/'Reader,'" which, for all its flirtations with theology, makes some crucial distinctions about how we do things with texts. See *George Steiner: A Reader* (New York: Oxford University Press), 67–98.

8. Louis Zukofsky, *A Test of Poetry* (New York: C.Z. Publications, 1980), vii.

9. Wallace Stevens, *Opus Posthumous,* ed. Samuel French Morse (New York: Knopf, 1957), 161.

10. Jerome J. McGann, "Response to Charles Altieri," in *Politics and Poetic Value,* ed. Robert Van Hallberg (Chicago: University of Chicago Press, 1987), 312. This volume also includes McGann's original essay on language poetry, "Contemporary Poetry, Alternate Routes," and Altieri's "Without Consequences Is No Politics: A Response to Jerome McGann." Altieri convincingly deflates some of the more naive political claims which McGann makes for language poetry; I am also suspicious of McGann's analogies between Romantic techniques and those of the language poets. On the other hand, McGann's analysis of language poetry as opposed to narrativity is quite useful.

11. Fredric Jameson, "Pleasure: A Political Issue," in *The Syntax of History,* vol. 2 of *The Ideologies of Theory* (Minneapolis: University of Minnesota Press, 1988), 74.

12. Michel Foucault, "The Discourse on Language," trans. Rupert Swyer, in *The Archaeology of Knowledge* (New York: Pantheon, 1972), 215.

13. Ibid.

14. Ibid., 216.

15. Ibid., 228.

16. Ibid., 220.

17. Michel Foucault, *The Order of Things* (New York: Pantheon, 1971), xviii.

18. Foucault, "The Discourse on Language," 219.

19. Ibid., 229.

20. Michel Foucault, "What Is an Author?," trans. Josue V. Harari, in *The Foucault Reader,* ed. Paul Rabinow (New York: Pantheon, 1984), 120.

21. Ibid., 102.

22. Ibid., 118.

23. Jacques Derrida, "Structure, Sign, and Play in the Discourse of the Human Sciences," in *The Structuralist Controversy,* ed. Richard Macksey and Eugenio Donato (Baltimore: Johns Hopkins University Press, 1972), 271.

24. Foucault, "What Is an Author?," 104.

25. Olivier Revault d'Allonnes, *Musical Variations On Jewish Thought,* trans. Judith L. Greenberg (New York: Braziller, 1984), 77–78.

26. Bernstein, *Content's Dream,* 34–35.

27. Bernstein, *Content's Dream,* 408–9.

28. Paul Smith, *Discerning the Subject* (Minneapolis: University of Minnesota Press, 1988), 5.

29. Bernstein, *Content's Dream*, 409.

30. Altieri, *Self and Sensibility*, 53.

31. McGann, "Contemporary Poetry, Alternate Routes," 275, 267.

32. Charles Bernstein, *Controlling Interests* (New York: Roof, 1980), 48.

33. Ibid., 49–50

34. Charles Bernstein, *Islets/Irritations* (New York: Jordan Davies, 1983), 74.

35. Zukofsky, *Prepositions*, 12.

36. Zukofsky, *All*, 133.

37. Bernstein, *Islets/Irritations*, 75.

38. Charles Bernstein, *The Sophist* (Los Angeles: Sun & Moon, 1987), 34.

39. Ibid., 35.

40. Ibid., 36.

41. Ron Silliman, *The New Sentence* (New York: Roof Books, 1989), 10.

42. Ibid., 17–18.

43. Ron Silliman, *Tjanting* (Great Barrington, Mass.: The Figures, 1981), 71. I randomly selected this passage from the text.

44. Perloff, *Dance of the Intellect*, 221.

45. Here I am arguing against Jerome McGann's view of *Tjanting*, which he contrasts with John Hollander's *Reflections on Espionage*, a work of "decadence" with roots in the late nineteenth century. For me, Silliman's attitude toward language makes him no less decadent than Hollander, however different his pedigree. See McGann, "Contemporary Poetry, Alternate Routes," 267–76.

46. T. S. Eliot, "What Is Minor Poetry," *On Poetry and Poets* (New York: Noonday Press, 1957), 36.

47. Foucault, "What Is an Author?," 101.

48. Altieri, *Self and Sensibility*, 64.

49. Robert Hass, *Twentieth Century Pleasures* (New York: Ecco Press, 1984), 152.

50. Robert Hass, *Praise* (New York: Ecco Press, 1979), 17.

51. For remarks indicating Palmer's similarities and differences to the language poets (such as Charles Bernstein, Ron Silliman, Lyn Hejinian, Barrett Watten, et al.), see Michael Palmer, "A Conversation," *American Poetry* 3, no. 1 (1986): 72–88. For my reading of Palmer, see Norman Finkelstein, "The Case of Michael Palmer," *Contemporary Literature* 29, no. 4 (Winter 1988): 518–37.

52. Michael Palmer, *Notes for Echo Lake* (San Francisco: North Point Press, 1981), 87.

53. The figure of the child learning verbal skills occupies a privileged place in Palmer's poetic world. See Norman Finkelstein, "Michael Palmer's Songs for Sarah," *Occident* 103, no. 1 (1990): 51–56.

54. Walter Benjamin, "On Language as Such and on the Language of Man," in *Reflections*, trans. Edmund Jephcott (New York: Schocken Books, 1986), 327.

55. Hass, *Praise*, 5.

56. Palmer, *Notes for Echo Lake*, 16.

Chapter 6. In the Fullness of Time

1. Bloch, *A Philosophy of the Future*, 96.

2. Ernst Bloch, *On Karl Marx*, trans. John Maxwell (New York: Herder and Herder, 1971), 38.

3. Bloch, *A Philosophy of the Future*, 124.

4. Benjamin, *Illuminations*, 262.

5. For a discussion of Bronk's notion of "the world" and other related themes, see Norman Finkelstein, "William Bronk: The World as Desire," *Contemporary Literature* 23, no. 4 (Fall 1982): 480–92.

6. William Bronk, *Life Supports: New and Collected Poems* (San Francisco: North Point Press, 1981), 48.

7. Ibid., 89.

8. Ibid., 39.

9. See Henry Weinfield, "The Poetry of William Bronk," *The Mysterious Barricades* 4 (Winter 1976): 51, for more on Bronk's relation to Ecclesiastes.

10. Bronk, *Life Supports*, 70.

11. Bronk has graciously informed me that the theme he is extending here comes from the last lines of Conrad's *Youth*. Marlow has finished his story, and the narrator concludes:

> And we all nodded at him: the man of finance, the man of accounts, the man of law, we all nodded at him over the polished table that like a still sheet of brown water reflected our faces, lined, wrinkled; our faces marked by toil, by deception, by success, by love; our weary eyes looking still, looking always, looking anxiously for something out of life, that while it is expected is already gone—has passed unseen, in a sigh, in a flash—together with the youth, with the strength, with the romance of illusions.

Such a work would obviously attract Bronk: Marlow's critical perspective on his youthful past, in the face of his more conventional listeners, more willing to accept illusions, augments Bronk's own view of the insufficiency of our temporal experience when compared to our desire.

12. Bronk, *Life Supports*, 179.

13. Cf. the long-standing dispute concerning the priority of poetry over historiography and philosophy, which may be traced at least as far back as Plato, is recapitulated in the Renaissance by Sidney in his *Apology of Poetry*, and is examined from a Marxist perspective by Terry Eagleton in *Criticism and Ideology*, 73–77.

14. William Bronk, *Vectors and Smoothable Curves: Collected Essays* (San Francisco: North Point Press, 1983), 14.

15. Ibid., 17.

16. Ibid., 18.

17. Ibid.

18. Ibid., 19–20.

19. Ibid., 34.

20. Ibid., 35.

21. Benjamin, *Illuminations*, 256.

22. Bronk, *Vectors*, 41.

23. Ibid., 42–43.

24. I am, of course, drawing upon the paradigm of the "right" and "left" interpretations of Hegel, which partly accounts for the development of Marx's early thought.

25. Bronk, *Life Supports*, 154.

26. Weinfield, "The Poetry of William Bronk," 51.

27. Bronk, *Life Supports*, 125.

28. Ibid., 140.

29. Ibid., 142.

30. Hudson, *Ernst Bloch*, 19–20.

31. Bronk, *Life Supports*, 153.

Conclusion: On Tradition

1. John Ashbery, *A Wave* (New York: Viking, 1984), 17.
2. Paul de Man, *Blindness and Insight*, 2d ed. (Minneapolis: University of Minnesota Press, 1983), 31.
3. Georg Lukács, *Marxism and Human Liberation*, ed. E. San Juan, Jr. (New York: Dell, 1973), 8.
4. See Gerald Graff, "Humanism and the Hermeneutics of Power: Reflections on the Post-Structuralist Two-Step and Other Dances," *Boundary 2* 12, no. 1 (Spring/Fall 1984): 495–505. The final piece in a special issue devoted largely to post-structuralist attacks on "the discourse of humanism," Graff's essay makes the crucial distinction between critiques of humanism from within its own boundaries and post-structuralist critiques from outside those boundaries, typified by the work of Michel Foucault. As should be clear by now, I see my own work as belonging to the former camp, subscribing to what Graff calls the "weak" version of the hermeneutics of power, in which "traditional forms of knowledge and culture are not discarded but liberated from their earlier social embodiments and put in the service of humanistic ends" (499).
5. Marshall Berman, *All That Is Solid Melts into Air: The Experience of Modernity* (New York: Simon and Schuster, 1982), 17.
6. De Man, *Blindness and Insight*, 152.
7. Ibid.
8. Ibid., 147.
9. Bernstein, "Robert Duncan," 181.
10. Ibid., 189.
11. Terry Eagleton, *Walter Benjamin*, 59.
12. Ibid., 48.
13. Gershom Scholem, *The Messianic Idea in Judaism* (New York: Schocken Books, 1971), 296.
14. Bronk, *Life Supports*, 25.

Appendix: Ernst Bloch and the Utopian Refunctioning of Marxism

1. Ernst Bloch, *The Utopian Function of Art and Literature*, trans. Jack Zipes and Frank Mecklenburg (Cambridge: MIT Press, 1988), 30.
2. Ibid., 27.
3. Ibid., 107.
4. Ibid., 275.
5. Ibid., 117–18.
6. Ibid., 52.
7. Ibid., 110.
8. Jameson, *Marxism and Form*, 137.
9. Bloch, *The Utopian Function*, 58.
10. Eagleton, *Criticism and Ideology*, 166–67.
11. Ibid., 69.
12. Jacques Derrida, "Structure, Sign, and Play," 250.
13. Jameson, *Marxism and Form*, 142.
14. Ibid., 119–20.
15. Hudson, *The Marxist Philosophy of Ernst Bloch*, 114.
16. Bloch, *The Utopian Function*, 162.
17. Jameson, *Marxism and Form*, 145.

18. Bloch, *The Utopian Function*, 126.

19. Cf. Jurgen Habermas, "Ernst Bloch: A Marxist Romantic," *Salmagundi* 10/11 (1969–1970): 316–18.

20. Anson Rabinbach, "Benjamin, Bloch and Modern German Jewish Messianism," *New German Critique* 34 (1985): 81.

21. Ibid.

22. See David Biale, *Gershom Scholem: Kabbalah and Counter-History* (Cambridge: Harvard University Press, 1979), 52–78, 148–88.

23. Rabinbach, "Jewish Messianism," 116.

24. Ibid., 113–14.

25. Scholem, *The Messianic Idea in Judaism*, 341.

26. Ibid., 45.

27. Bloch, *The Utopian Function*, 153.

28. Habermas, "Ernst Bloch," 317.

29. Bloch, *The Utopian Function*, 170.

30. Ibid., 259.

31. Ibid., xxii.

32. Hudson, *Ernst Bloch*, 96.

33. Milan Kundera, *Life Is Elsewhere*, trans. Peter Kussi (New York: Penguin, 1986), 270.

34. Ibid., vi. Also, see Kundera's remarks in *The Book of Laughter and Forgetting*, trans. Michael Henry Heim (New York: Penguin, 1981), 65–68.

35. Bloch, *The Utopian Function*, 158.

36. Ibid., 159.

37. Kundera, *Book of Laughter and Forgetting*, 66.

38. Bloch, *The Utopian Function*, 162.

39. Fredric Jameson, "Postmodernism, or The Cultural Logic of Late Capitalism," *New Left Review* 146 (1984): 62 and *passim*.

40. Bloch, *The Utopian Function*, 160.

41. Jameson, "Postmodernism," 63–64.

42. Bloch, *The Utopian Function*, 160–61.

43. Ibid., 118.

44. Ibid., 48.

45. Terry Eagleton, *Against the Grain: Essays 1975–1985* (London: Verso, 1986), 77.

Works Cited

Primary Sources

Adam, Helen. *Gone Sailing*. West Branch, Iowa: The Toothpaste Press, 1980.

————.*Selected Poems & Ballads*. New York: Helekon Press, 1974.

————.*Turn Again to Me & Other Poems*. New York: Kulchur Foundation, 1977.

Ashbery, John. *As We Know*. New York: Penguin, 1979.

————. *The Double Dream of Spring*. New York: E. P. Dutton & Co., 1970.

————. *Houseboat Days*. New York: Penguin, 1977.

————. *Rivers and Mountains*. New York: Holt Rinehart Winston, 1966.

————. *Self-Portrait in a Convex Mirror*. New York: Penguin, 1975.

————. *Some Trees*. 1956. Reprint. New York: Ecco Press, 1978.

————. *A Wave*. New York: Viking Press, 1984.

Bronk, William. *Life Supports: New and Collected Poems*. San Francisco: North Point Press, 1981.

————. *Vectors and Smoothable Curves: Collected Essays*. San Francisco: North Point Press, 1983.

Duncan, Robert. *Bending the Bow*. New York: New Directions, 1968.

————. *Fictive Certainties*. New York: New Directions, 1985.

————. *Ground Work: Before the War*. New York: New Directions, 1984.

————. *The Opening of the Field*. New York: New Directions. 1960.

————. *The Years as Catches*. Berkeley, Calif.: Oyez Press, 1966.

Feld, Ross. *Plum Poems*. New York: Jargon Society, 1972.

Johnson, Ronald. *Ark: The Foundations*. San Francisco: North Point Press, 1980.

————. *The Book of the Green Man*. New York: W. W. Norton, 1967.

————. *Radi Os*. Albany, Calif.: Sand Dollar Press, 1977.

————. *The Valley of the Many-Colored Grasses*. New York: Norton, 1969.

O'Hara, Frank. *The Collected Poems of Frank O'Hara*. Edited by Donald Allen. New York: Alfred A. Knopf, 1971.

Oppen, George. *Collected Poems*. New York: New Directions, 1975.

Spicer, Jack. *The Collected Poems of Jack Spicer*. Edited by Robin Blaser. Los Angeles: Black Sparrow Press, 1975.

Stevens, Wallace. *The Collected Poems of Wallace Stevens*. New York: Alfred A. Knopf, 1956.

Williams, William Carlos. *Collected Earlier Poems of William Carlos Williams.* New York: New Directions, 1951.

———. *Imaginations.* Edited by Webster Schott. New York: New Directions, 1970.

———. *Selected Essays.* New York: New Directions, 1954.

Zukofsky, Louis. *"A".* Berkeley: University of California Press, 1978.

———. *All: The Collected Short Poems.* New York: W. W. Norton, 1971.

———. *Prepositions: The Collected Critical Essays of Louis Zukofsky.* Berkeley: University of California Press, 1981.

Secondary Sources

Adorno, Theodor. *Prisms.* Translated by Samuel and Shierry Weber. Cambridge: MIT Press, 1981.

Ahearn, Barry. *Zukofsky's "A".* Berkeley: University of California Press, 1983.

Altieri, Charles. *Enlarging the Temple.* Lewisburg, Pa.: Bucknell University Press, 1979.

———. "The Objectivist Tradition." *Chicago Review* 30, no. 3 (Winter 1979): 5–22.

———. *Self and Sensibility in Contemporary American Poetry.* Cambridge: Cambridge University Press, 1984.

Auden, W. H. *The English Auden.* Edited by Edward Mendelson. New York: Random House, 1977.

Benjamin, Walter. *Illuminations.* Translated by Harry Zohn. New York: Schocken Books, 1968.

Berman, Marshall. *All That Is Solid Melts into Air: The Experience of Modernity.* New York: Simon and Schuster, 1982.

Bertholf, Robert J., and Ian W. Reid. *Robert Duncan: Scales of the Marvelous.* New York: New Directions, 1979.

Bloch, Ernst. *Man on His Own.* Translated by E. G. Ashton. New York: Herder and Herder, 1970.

———. *A Philosophy of the Future.* Translated by John Cumming. New York: Herder and Herder, 1970.

Bloom, Harold. *Figures of Capable Imagination.* New York: The Seabury Press, 1976.

Breslin, James E. *From Modern to Contemporary: American Poetry 1945–1965.* Chicago: University of Chicago Press, 1984.

Burke, Kenneth. *A Grammar of Motives and A Rhetoric of Motives.* Cleveland, Ohio: World Publishing Co., 1962.

———. *The Philosophy of Literary Form.* 2d ed. Baton Rouge: Louisiana State University Press, 1967.

Byrd, Don. "The Poetry of Production." *Sagetrieb* 2, no. 2 (Summer/Fall 1983): 7–43.

Creeley, Robert. *A Quick Graph: Collected Notes & Essays.* Edited by Donald Allen. San Francisco: Four Seasons Foundation, 1970.

Davenport, Guy. *The Geography of the Imagination.* San Francisco: North Point Press, 1981.

de Man, Paul. *Blindness and Insight*. 2d ed. Minneapolis: University of Minnesota Press, 1983.

Dembo, L. S., and Cyrena N. Pondrom. *The Contemporary Writer*. Madison: University of Wisconsin Press, 1972.

Dinnerstein, Dorothy. *The Mermaid and the Minotaur: Sexual Arrangements and Human Malaise*. New York: Harper & Row, 1976.

Eagleton, Terry. *Criticism and Ideology*. London: NLB, 1976.

———. "Fredric Jameson: The Politics of Style." *Diacritics* 12, no. 3 (Fall 1982): 14–22.

———. *Walter Benjamin or Towards a Revolutionary Criticism*. London: NLB, 1981.

Feldman, Alan. *Frank O'Hara*. Boston: Twayne, 1979.

Freud, Sigmund. *Civilization and Its Discontents*. Vol. 21 in *The Standard Edition of the Complete Works of Sigmund Freud*. Translated by James Strachey. London: The Hogarth Press, 1961.

Frye, Northrop. *The Anatomy of Criticism: Four Essays*. Princeton: Princeton University Press, 1957.

Graff, Gerald. "Humanism and the Hermeneutics of Power: Reflections on the Post-Structuralist Two-Step and Other Dances." *Boundary 2* 12, no. 1 (Spring/Fall 1984): 495–505.

———. *Literature against Itself: Literary Ideas in Modern Society*. Chicago: University of Chicago Press, 1979.

Harmon, William. "The Poetry of a Journal at the End of an Arbor in a Watch." *Parnassus* 9, no. 1 (Spring/Summer 1981): 217–32.

Hatlen, Burton, ed. *George Oppen: Man & Poet*. Orono, Maine: National Poetry Foundation, 1981.

———. Review of *The Postmoderns*, edited by Donald Allen and George Butterick. *Sagetrieb* 1, no. 2 (Fall 1982): 325–28.

Hornick, Lita. "The Haunted Land of Helen Adam." *Sun & Moon* 9/10 (Summer 1980): 138–41.

Hudson, Wayne. *The Marxist Philosophy of Ernst Bloch*. New York: St. Martin's Press, 1982.

Jameson, Fredric. *Marxism and Form*. Princeton: Princeton University Press, 1971.

———. *The Political Unconscious*. Ithaca: Cornell University Press, 1981.

Jauss, Hans Robert. *Toward an Aesthetic of Reception*. Translated by Timothy Bahti. Minneapolis: University of Minnesota Press, 1982.

Kenner, Hugh. *A Homemade World*. New York: Alfred A. Knopf, 1975.

Kermode, Frank. *Romantic Image*. New York: Vintage Books, 1964.

Lehman, David. ed. *Beyond Amazement: New Essays on John Ashbery*. Ithaca: Cornell University Press, 1980.

Lukács, Georg. *Marxism and Human Liberation*. Edited by E. San Juan, Jr. New York: Dell Publishing Co., 1973.

———. *The Theory of the Novel*. Translated by Anna Bostock. Cambridge: MIT Press, 1971.

Manuel, Frank E., and Fritzie P. Manuel. *Utopian Thought in the Western World*. Cambridge: Harvard University Press, 1979.

Marx, Karl, and Friedrich Engels. *The German Ideology.* Edited by C. J. Arthur. New York: International Publishers, 1970.

Molesworth, Charles. *The Fierce Embrace.* Columbia: University of Missouri Press, 1979.

Newman, Charles. *The Post-Modern Aura: The Act of Fiction in an Age of Inflation.* Evanston, Ill.: Northwestern University Press, 1985.

Olson, Charles. *Human Universe & Other Essays.* Edited by Donald Allen. New York: Grove Press, 1967.

Palmer, Michael, ed. *Code of Signals: Recent Writings in Poetics.* Berkeley, Calif.: North Atlantic Books, 1983.

Perloff, Marjorie. *Frank O'Hara: Poet among Painters.* New York: George Braziller, 1977.

———. *The Poetics of Indeterminacy.* Princeton: Princeton University Press, 1981.

Rothenberg, Jerome. "Keeping It Old: A Review of the New *New American Poetry.*" *Sulfur* 6 (1983): 181–90.

Scholem, Gershom. *The Messianic Idea in Judaism.* New York: Schocken Books, 1971.

Slaughter, Cliff. *Marxism, Ideology and Literature.* Atlantic Highlands, N.J.: Humanities Press, 1980.

Terrell, C. F., ed. *Louis Zukofsky: Man & Poet.* Orono, Maine: National Poetry Foundation, 1979.

———. *William Carlos Williams: Man & Poet.* Orono, Maine: National Poetry Foundation, 1983.

Trotsky, Leon. *Literature and Revolution.* Translated by Rose Strunsky. Ann Arbor: University of Michigan Press, 1960.

Von Hallberg, Robert. *American Poetry and Culture 1945–1980.* Cambridge: Harvard University Press, 1985.

———. "The Politics of Description: W. C. Williams in the 'Thirties." *ELH* 45 (1978): 131–51.

Von Hallberg, Robert, ed. *Canons.* Chicago: University of Chicago Press, 1984.

Weinfield, Henry. "The Poetry of William Bronk." *The Mysterious Barricades* 4 (Winter 1976): 47–51.

Williamson, Alan. *Introspection and Contemporary Poetry.* Cambridge: Harvard University Press, 1984.

Yeats, W. B. *Essays and Introductions.* New York: Macmillan Publishing Co., 1961.

———. *Mythologies.* New York: Macmillan, 1959.

Index